The Secrets Of Innovational Leadership

100 Points That Light The Path To The Future

Gary Francis Chaplin
Chaplin Consulting Services LLC

This book is dedicated to the inventive spirit of mankind and those who exemplify man's best attributes in the great cause of advancing the well-being of all of the people on this planet.

Preface

It takes a combination of curiosity, imagination, ideas, and logic to formulate an innovative concept and product, and it requires strong leadership to bring it to fruition. This book is written to assist in the development of that innovative sprit and leadership. It is written in a unique format that is intended to be an enhanced, simplified, innovative, and enjoyable approach to information sharing. Rather than containing just black and white printed words of guidance on leadership and innovation, the book integrates and displays the beauty, diversity, and innovative life found in the natural world around us.

The book is organized into 10 chapters with 10 sections in each. It takes you from the vision, the team, the strategies, the product, the attributes, the actions, and the behaviors of a leader to a projection of the future. Each chapter has an introduction followed by 10 discussion points. Each discussion point, or point of light, occupies one page. Each page has a title that speaks to a leadership attribute. It has a brief description of the attribute and its relevance to innovation. There is a quote from a well-known person to support that thought. Where appropriate, there is a picture taken in the natural world that conveys the basic thought. The verbiage is kept to a minimum, and the book concentrates on a straight forward presentation of the fundamentals of innovational leadership.

A picture can be worth a thousand words and can best elicit our emotions and feelings, so for some points, there is a picture to reinforce the thought that is presented. These pictures of birds, and one picture of the Andromeda Galaxy(M31), were taken in the natural world by the author and his wife. Birds such as the eagle, vulture, owl, and turkey have come to represent well recognized human behavior; more importantly, birds are an embodiment of man's ancient dreams of flight, travel, adventure, and freedom. Many familiar expressions of reaching for the unknown involve flying and will be explored in this book.

Birds accomplish great journeys of migration across vast expanses of this planet. They fly in "V" formations that enhance this capability and depend on the leader for direction, persistence, and endurance. Tracing their ancestry back 50 million years to the dinosaurs, they have evolved to a design of beauty, grace, and function. Their hollow bones, light weight feathers, and aerodynamic wings and body are an example of a simple, elegant, and functionally innovative systems design. Einstein said: *"Look deep into nature, and then you will understand everything better."*

The innovations we create need to fit harmoniously into the natural world around us. The Earth is a precious place, unique in the solar system, and the only celestial body that will support human life as we know it. We need to appreciate and protect its beauty, its wildlife, and its sustaining processes while we utilize its resources for our innovations and the benefit of mankind.

The quotes are by recognized innovators, pioneers, philosophers, and leaders: Aesop, Aristotle, Neil Armstrong, Alexander Graham Bell, Dr. Wernher Von Braun, George Washington Carver, Sir Winston Churchill, Confucius, Marie Curie, Walt Disney, Amelia Earhart, Thomas Edison, Dwight D. Eisenhower, Albert Einstein, Ralph Waldo Emerson, Henry Ford, Benjamin Franklin, Indira Gandhi, Mahatma Gandhi, Robert Goddard, Patrick Henry, Soichiro Honda, Thomas Jefferson, Steve Jobs, Clarence L. "Kelly" Johnson, Lord Kelvin, John F. Kennedy, Dr. Martin Luther King, Edwin H. Land, Leonardo da Vinci, Abraham Lincoln, Charles Lindbergh, Vince Lombardi, Henry Wadsworth Longfellow, Akio Morita, Sir Isaac Newton, David Packard, Thomas Paine, George S. Patton, Frederick B. Rentschler, Eleanor Roosevelt, Franklin Roosevelt, Theodore Roosevelt, Babe Ruth, Dr. Jonas

Salk, Igor Sikorsky, Henry David Thoreau, Jules Verne, George Washington, and Wilbur Wright. There are 50 different people who are quoted. However, Churchill, Disney, Edison, Einstein, Franklin, and Theodore Roosevelt are quoted five or more times. Their ability to express powerful thoughts with great emotion, using the fewest words, was what set them apart for the purposes of this book.

There is a self-improvement test at the end of the book. There are 10 chapters, each with 10 discussion points, for a total of 100 discussion points. If you feel that you have achieved the discussion point's behavior or recommendation, you score it a "yes." A perfect score would be a "yes" to each point, or 100 "yeses" equal 100%. This section is intended to help you focus on areas that you can improve and strengthen.

The book is written to support innovational leadership at all levels, from the CEO, to the individual contributor on an innovation team, to the lone entrepreneur. Above all the book is meant to be enjoyed; for leadership is a natural skills process that we all need to employ and improve in our daily lives.

Contents

Part 1.
Developing A Vision

Before you can lead an innovation team you must have a vision of an improved future state. You start developing visions by being curious and asking questions about the products and processes around you. You use your imagination in generating ideas for improvements. Pour these ideas through your logic filters and come up with a creative thought. A synergistic combination of these creative thoughts then leads to more practical innovations that you can test against reality of what exists today. From your vision you can develop a strategy for implementation. These innovations may improve existing products and processes, or they may create new industries.

Thomas Edison had a vision that man could record and play back the human voice. The Wright Brothers had a vision that controlled flight was possible for man. Walt Disney had a vision of a theme park that he could take his daughters to for a fun filled family outing. Steve Jobs had a vision of a personal computer in every home, a bicycle of the mind. George Washington Carver had a vision of a South that was free from its dependence on the cotton crop. Each of these people overcame great obstacles to turn their ideas and dreams into a reality that benefited all mankind. This book is dedicated to continuing their innovative spirit by capturing their approaches and methodologies, along with those of other great innovators and leaders of change, to help you turn your visions into reality.

Regarding your vision, the initial thought process should focus on how the innovation you will provide will have a positive effect on changing the world and improving people's lives, and not only economically. In a speech to HP managers, David Packard expresses it this way: *"I think many people assume, wrongly, that a company exists simply to make money. -- a group of people get together and exist as -- a company so they are able to accomplish something collectively which they could not accomplish separately. -- they make a contribution to society."*

Focus first and foremost on achieving world leadership. Frederick B. Rentschler, the founder of Pratt & Whitney Division of UTC, where I worked for 31 years, set the target for all who would follow—*"The forward objective is clear cut and no less than obtaining world leadership in aviation power plants."* Every time we followed this vision, market success and profit followed.

In this section, the need to focus your vision on the goal of world leadership is presented along with supporting discussion points.

Discussion Points

1. Aim Your Product Goal At World Leadership
2. Be A Visionary Dreamer
3. Dedicate Time For Imagination & Fantasy
4. Choose A New Direction
5. Leap Frog The Competition
6. Present Your Vision
7. Overcome The Initial Resistance To Change
8. Recognize The Tipping Point
9. Stay Customer Focused
10. Vision + Daring + Conviction = Success

Aim Your Product Goal At World Leadership

The main goal is not about making money. The primary focus needs to be world leadership in the product hardware and software, and in processes employed to deliver it. With this in mind, financial success will follow.

It's all about changing the world and making a better life for all the people on this planet. One only has to look at the positive impact of Apple products on people's lives, and that they are one of the world's most valuable companies. Innovators like Thomas Edison, Walt Disney, and Steve Jobs have changed the world and made it a better place, while at the same time creating highly profitable enterprises.

Create for yourself a responsible and lofty future vision: allow yourself to soar above the waves. Ahead lies world leadership.

" The virtuous man is driven by responsibility, the non-virtuous man is driven by profit."

Confucius

Be A Visionary Dreamer

You are a leader because you have had a dream, a vision of an improved future state that you wish to turn into a reality. You have let your imagination soar and you have an idea for an innovative product or process that you need to make real.

In your mind's eye you can see this new product in use, setting new standards of excellence, and achieving a level of performance well beyond what others think is possible or appropriate. Or perhaps you can see it creating a new industry.

Two bicycle mechanics from Ohio had a dream that flight was possible for man. They separated lift from thrust, built gliders, then ventured into power flight. They found the lift equations of the day to be inaccurate, but they didn't give up their dream. They rewrote the lift equations and tested new lift concepts until their glider was perfected. There did not exist an engine of the required thrust to weight ratio, so undaunted, they designed their own. The next year they built the engine and took their powered glider to Kitty Hawk, North Carolina, and fulfilled man's oldest dream.

Dreaming plays an essential role in innovation. Stand above the crowd and allow yourself to dream. Dreamers change the world.

"Let us not forget it has been the visionary dreamers who have accomplished more for the edification and benefit of mankind than any other contributor to civilization past or present."

Dr. Wernher Von Braun

Dedicate Time For Imagination & Fantasy

You must let your imagination soar to think out of the box and achieve a breakthrough vision. It is important to allow yourself time during the day for fantasy and dreams of a better tomorrow. The fantasy is then combined with the reality, where you can see the true benefits of the concept, and the challenges and unknowns that must be surmounted.

It is helpful to have a quiet thinking place and to record your best thoughts. Know your body rhythms and pick the time of the day that's best for you. Let the past, present, and future blend together like the colors in a rainbow. Free your mind to lead you to a new tomorrow.

"When I examine myself and my methods of thought I come to the conclusion that the gift of fantasy has meant more to me than my ability to absorb positive knowledge."

Albert Einstein

Choose A New Direction

You can't conform to the status quo if you are to break new ground. You can't stay in the comfort zone of those around you. You will be proposing a potentially revolutionary product or service that will change people's lives.

This new product will offer new technological utility that will make existing products and systems obsolete and will upset the future plans of your competition. There will be surprises on this new path, and that will make others uncomfortable. It is important to anticipate the resistance you will face, understand its origins, and forge ahead.

You can't fly with the flock if you are to set a new standard of excellence. Rise up and strike off in a new direction and open up new opportunities.

"Go confidently in the direction of your dreams. Live the life you have imagined."

Henry David Thoreau

Leap-Frog The Competition

Unburden yourself from suffocating constraints and ground rules that limit true progress. Your innovation will set a new standard of value through the technology, quality, and service you will provide. It is a synergistic combination of current and advanced technology that achieves metrics that far exceed those of others.

Snow White was not just another cartoon. It was a full-length animated movie, with fully developed characters possessing emotions that the audience could identify with. The three dimensional appearance of the characters was made possible by Disney invented technology: the multi-plane camera. It was called a true master piece, far beyond what other studios could achieve.

Disneyland was not just another amusement park, it was a theme park of unheard of size and scope. It was so far ahead of the rest of the industry it had no initial competition. It raised the bar and set a new standard for family vacation entertainment. I don't know anyone who has not taken their family to a Disney theme park.

Your innovation should not be aimed at achieving parity with the competition, but rather should be aimed at leaping over them. This bold approach will involve taking and managing risk, and overcoming challenges that you will surely face.

" Far better it is to dare mighty things, to win glorious triumphs, even though checkered by failure, than to take rank with those poor spirits who neither enjoy much or suffer much, because they live in the gray twilight that knows not victory nor defeat."

Theodore Roosevelt

Present Your Vision

After developing the vision, we need to present it with passion and conviction. To secure support for a radical new idea and change people's world view, you need to be respectful of the prior art, realistic about the challenges to overcome, and optimistic about the idea's future. Anticipating future customer needs and going well beyond their current expectations by launching new products and services is how to drive change and achieve world leadership.

Combine your imagination and creativity with your gut feelings and intuition and present a vision of a better future state. This is not the time for cautious words; there is always opposition to change. Don't be conservative; walk out on the limb and be optimistic.

"I feel that I have at last struck the solution of a great problem -- and the day is coming when telegraph(telephone) wires will be laid on to houses just like water or gas -- and friends converse with each other without leaving home."

Alexander Graham Bell

Overcome The Initial Resistance To Change

Most great ideas and innovations face stiff resistance when they are first introduced. This is to be expected. Edison's electric light bulb faced resistance from gas companies that provided gas powered lighting. They claimed electricity was too dangerous to be fed into people's homes. The Wright brothers were told by some of the leading experts of the day that heavier than air flying-machines were not possible. Walt Disney had a difficult time convincing banks to make a loan for Disneyland.

You will need disciples to help you sell your idea. Walt depended on his brother Roy's financial expertise, which included innovative deal making with potential supporters. To enlist the support of the ABC network for Disneyland, the Disney brothers agreed to produce TV programs for the network. It was a win-win for both companies.

Selling your idea involves plenty of leg work and "one-on-ones" prior to engaging in formal meetings. Meet with people and explain and defend your idea passionately. Use logic, facts, and good judgment when responding to criticism. You will receive good recommendations that should be incorporated in your vision and innovation. In this way, you will create a win-win scenario and turn the opposition into supporters in the formal meetings to follow. Still, some will reject your idea and turn away. Don't let that stop you.

"I could never convince the financiers that Disneyland was feasible, because dreams offer too little collateral."

Walt Disney

Recognize The Tipping Point

Some people, at first mention, resist almost any change— be it evolutionary, radical, and game changing or not. The good news is you don't need everyone's initial agreement when you first present an innovative project or vision. Evidence suggests that you only need to initially get the buy-in of 16% of the players before the others will follow. These early "adopters"/"evolvers" will help you expand the support for the idea. They will be your first disciples.

There was a structural issue in a very thin airfoil of a developmental engine, and I was asked to lead a team to fix this problem. The solution my team proposed was a damper to reduce vibration. This was strongly opposed by the structural experts, who took the position that a damper can't solve an aerodynamic problem, and the damper itself would not be durable. But as failures of the airfoil continued, one lead-development test engineer, who believed in the damper's potential, manufactured it and ran it. Stresses were so low that the airfoil never failed again. The damper was patented and became the production standard. This one person, the early "evolver," was all it took to get the idea into production.

Throw your chest out, be steadfast and show confidence in your idea while defending it. The facts and logic are on your side. Remain cool, calm, and collected under fire. Then, with the support of the "evolvers," momentum will build and tip in your favor.

===

"The evolvers are people who cause things to change. The maintainers of the status quo do everything to keep things from changing. The numbers of evolvers are much fewer than the maintainers of the status quo --"

Dr. Jonas Salk

Stay Customer Focused

Your innovation may be meeting a known customer need, or it may be creating a new industry. Either way, you will be depending on customer acceptance of your innovation. Keep in mind the end user experience. Build a prototype and let select customers try it out. Then modify it based on their input.

The innovation must offer a combination of technology, quality, and service, that when divided by the cost, yields a big leap in product value. Concentrate on your unique skills, on doing what others in the industry cannot do. The customers are looking to you to anticipate their future needs. You know you have achieved success when the new product experience you have delivered has satisfied the toughest customers in the market.

Henry Ford developed a concept for a "peoples" car. Before Ford, the cars being manufactured were basically handmade by frame and engine manufacturers with a custom body added later. They were aimed at the very rich. But Ford's idea was revolutionary, he would build a car for the average working American family. He conceived and built a mass-produced car of the simplest, lowest cost, and most durable design, the Model T. You could have it in any color, as long as that color was black.

"I will build a car for the great multitude. It will be large enough for the family, but small enough for the individual to run and take care of. It will be constructed of the best materials, by the best men --, after the simplest designs. But it will be so low in price that no man making a good salary will be unable to own one --"

Henry Ford

Vision + Daring + Conviction = Success

You have put your faith in the value proposition of this new product and made the bold decision to launch the project and to bring it to market. You have overcome the initial obstacles and gained a small group of supporting disciples and start-up financing.

The energy, enthusiasm, and conviction that you display in support of the project will be contagious. The stronger your will to succeed, the more persistent you will be in the face of adversities, the more unwilling to lose, the more likely the success.

The Wright brothers knew they were taking on their era's standard of human impossibility: "It can't be done, a man may as well try to fly." But, they reasoned, birds, bats, and insects fly; therefore, man might also fly. They had vision, daring, and a conviction of success and made that great leap forward.

" For some years I have been afflicted with the belief that flight is possible to man. My disease has increased in severity and I feel it will soon cost me an increased amount of money if not my life."

Wilbur Wright

Part 2.
Establishing An Innovation Team

You need to establish a team that will turn a vision into reality. This team will work well together and their skills will complement each other. Thomas Edison formed such a team at his Menlo Park innovation lab, and Walt Disney did the same at his studio.

Edison had a team of diverse and complementary talents. Ideas could be turned into equations that defined the physics of the solution by mathematician and physicist, Francis Upton. A simple sketch could be turned into a working model or prototype apparatus by John Kruesi. The manufacturing was placed in the hands of skilled machinist, John Ott. He depended on his chief experimental and technical assistant, Charles Batchelor, to coordinate the effort and convert the innovations into saleable products. This was a team of responsibility centers that operated without barriers and with completely open communications.

The team needs to supplement any of your weak areas. Walt's brother, Roy, was the person he turned to for financial expertise while Walt concentrated on the creative side of the business.

You need to select people of high integrity so that you can build trust between each team member and yourself. When you have trust, you don't need creativity stifling bureaucracy.

It is your responsibility as team leader to know each person's capabilities and match these to the job at hand. Then you must build a synergy of all these individual efforts into a team effort aligned toward the goal. The result will be an innovative system and product that is greater than the sum of its parts.

Discussion Points

1. Turn Vision Into Action
2. Select A Team Of High Integrity
3. Treat Every Team Member As Important
4. Build A Team of Diverse & Creative Thinkers
5. Create Responsibility Centers
6. Match Peoples Skills To Their Assignments
7. Respect Cultural Differences
8. Assure Team Alignment
9. Optimize Teamwork
10. Achieve A Synergy of Team Effort

Turn Vision Into Action

Hope is not a strategy; you can't just hope for a better future. You need to have both a vision and a plan of action to get there. You need a strategy and tactics to back it up. In most cases your vision can not be accomplished on your own within a reasonable time frame. You'll need to establish a strong team of empowered and dedicated individuals to help form, enhance, and execute the vision. With a team in hand, you can divide the required effort into manageable tasks, and by working in parallel, the vision will become a reality much faster.

You don't want to wait until you have all the pieces of your new concept together to form an action team. You want the team to contribute to the concept and acquire the ownership that comes from early participation. Since the concept phase of a project is the most important, you must form your team as early as possible. The key is to get buy-in and commitment from every team member at the concept phase. Then, when the inevitable issues arise during development, they will not walk away but will persevere to overcome them.

You need to add people from disciplines that will enhance your own capabilities, particularly in those areas that are not your greatest strengths. If your innovation is going to change the world, you will need world-class experts in all the relevant fields

See the improved future state and acquire action-oriented, results driven people to make it happen.

"Vision without action is a daydream. Action without vision is a nightmare."

Japanese Proverb

Select A Team Of High Integrity

A team must fly in close formation where dedication, training, and skill are interwoven. The first thing leaders do is put a strong team in place that will support their vision and reflect their ethics, but one that will also challenge them on strategy. You need their honest criticism so the project will be successful. After thorough discussion of all points, and the inclusion of their best recommendations, all team members should be aligned to support the decisions made.

Formation flying requires discipline. Discipline is created by the systems and processes you put in place to guide the project. When you have discipline, you don't need bureaucracy and excess paperwork. Your success, and the success of the project, depends on the performance of your team members. You need people you trust to be your wingmen.

" Associate yourself with men of good quality if you esteem your own reputation for 'tis better to be alone than in bad company."

George Washington

Treat Every Team Member As Important

A chain is only as strong as its weakest link, and each link is required to perform its full function. Every job assignment is not of equal difficulty, but all are important. Each person on the team deserves a thoughtful assignment and the resources to succeed in their pursuit of excellence.

Most innovative products involve the synergy of many technologies. This can be attained only by having skilled people in each of the required disciplines. These people, although from different disciplines, will need to integrate their capabilities to evolve the best concept solution that meets the product's goals. One person not performing their function will be a bottleneck in the required timely flow of information. You will need world class people in each discipline.

As you interview each person for your team, you must be certain that they are the right fit for the challenge you plan to put before them. Tell them the truth up front and have an honest conversation about your expectations, and theirs.

Visit with each person on your team often to understand their challenges and progress. Be supportive while providing guidance toward the group's goal. In this way they will realize their importance. The last person you add to complete the team is as important as the first person brought on board.

"If it falls to your lot to be a street sweeper, -- sweep the streets like Michelangelo painted pictures, -- and Beethoven composed music, -- sweep the streets so well that all the hosts of heaven and earth will have to pause and say: Here lived a great street sweeper who sweep his job well."

Dr. Martin Luther King

Build A Team of Diverse & Creative Thinkers

Your team should represent all the disciplines required to do the job. It should include people who are capable in areas you are not. You are looking for people who can think out of the box, have energy and enthusiasm, and are self-motivated. They should not be "yes" people, but should challenge you in an open environment, where in the end, you still make the final judgment.

This team will not dress alike, look alike, talk alike, or think alike. They will have their eccentricities, and this will result in a continuous flow of ideas and approaches to problems. A diverse team will assure all approaches to the challenge are carefully explored.

You don't want a chorus of the same old ideas, reflecting the thoughts of a single discipline, to be the response to a challenging question.

"No one is thinking if everyone is thinking alike."

George S. Patton

Create Responsibility Centers

The major deliverables that you own need to be assigned to your team members. You can't be everywhere making all the local decisions in a timely fashion yourself. You need to define the results required and hold them accountable. It is essential to monitor the progress being made toward the results, for in the end, you are responsible for them.

Measurable deliverables like cost, weight, performance, and reliability are good examples of metrics that need to be monitored and driven home throughout the program. The team member responsible for each deliverable should share your passion and be striving for positive results. They should not be just metric status reporters. They should fully understand the objective and use their own ingenuity in achieving the target goal. Success lies in the capturing of this challenging metric target.

In addition to the drive to achieve the product metrics, you will also need to assign responsibility for the supporting technology development efforts that you are counting on. Failure to monitor technology programs can result in missed delivery dates and costly retrofits.

There will be problem areas, and it is on those that you should weigh in and provide assistance to the responsibility center owners as needed.

"We feel our objectives can best be achieved by people who understand what they are trying to do and can utilize their own capabilities to do them."

David Packard

Match Peoples Skills To
Their Assignments

Work closely with your team members so that you can position them for success. If they are not right for a particular assignment, change it and create a better match. Everyone has skill and value to contribute if we position them to succeed.

Understand each person's special capabilities and future vision, and don't let a person fail. It is hurtful to them, disruptive to the job, and a lose-lose scenario. When people have the right job match, they can't wait to tackle the next assignment. They take pride in their work and become strong contributors with a can-do attitude.

Nature provides each living creature with special skills and equips them to thrive, as with the unique fish catching bill of the Brown Pelican. When all have the right assignment, then aim them at the target goal.

"Of all the things I've done, the most vital is coordinating those who work with me and aiming their efforts at a certain goal."

Walt Disney

Respect Cultural Differences

No one country or culture has a monopoly on all the best approaches to life and work. Every team project with international partners is an opportunity to significantly expand your knowledge of the best products, processes, technology, and people in your industry.

Meetings with international partners will involve additional travel time, jet lag, language translations, and precise documentation of decisions. Strong leadership is required to overcome these obstacles and to assure that the key issues are put on the table, decisions are made, documented, and carried out.

A strengthened systems integration team will be needed to assure careful control of component hardware and software interfaces. When the key components of a product are manufactured in different countries, there is a high risk that they will not fit together and perform as intended without additional interface control effort and resources. We have seen this happen with high-profile products in the aviation industry, thereby costing the manufacturer billions of dollars.

Go out of your way to show respect for your international team members and you will be well served by them while making partnerships for a lifetime. You will find that common purpose and the desire for project success outweigh any cultural differences.

"Mutual respect is the basis of all civilized human relationships -- it is a requirement in the work one does with one's associates -- it is increasingly necessary in seeking cooperation among the peoples of the world."

Eleanor Roosevelt

Assure Team Alignment

This is a team of strong willed individuals and you must let them all feel free to explore their innovative side, and yet all must be pulling in one direction to achieve the desired product outcome. There will be a product systems team leader, and there will be component team leaders for the subsystems. All components must be optimized with the realization that it is their functioning in the product system that has the highest priority.

The systems team leader must see that all the component leaders are kept up to date and aligned to the latest in program requirements, and that their primary focus is on achieving the product goals. We don't want sub-optimization of components at the expense of the product.

The component team leader must see that each team member knows their role and responsibility for the team's overall success. Each member must know they're important and that the team cannot succeed without them. The more time you share talking and listening with each team member, the stronger the bond of common purpose, and the greater the alignment.

Individual sticks can be easily broken, but a bundle of aligned sticks has great strength, as Aesop pointed out in the fable *The Bundle of Sticks*. There is great strength derived from unity of purpose. Keep all the members of your team aligned to the target and achieve the strength and synergy of a number-one team effort.

" United we stand: divided we fall."

Aesop

Optimize Teamwork

Team exercises build strength and unity of purpose. Offsite meetings that encourage understanding and commitment to group goals and include team building exercises are a valuable tool. These should be led by a skilled facilitator.

The offsite location takes people away from their daily emails, regular meetings, and normal routine. Now they can mingle with other leaders, and understand better how their part of the project effects the whole system's result. They have time to think out of the box, and entertain solutions that might otherwise be missed.

In a small team, each member should get a turn to speak to the group about their vision to accomplish both their individual aims, and the overall team goals. An open discussion of potential issues and solutions should follow. Your team will leave these exercises with confidence in both the direction they're going, and the people they will depend on as they chase the team's goals.

You should set the tone for the meeting with your opening remarks, as Vince Lombardi did in his opening remarks at his first team meeting as Green Bay Packers head coach.

"Gentleman, we are going to relentlessly chase perfection, knowing full well we will not catch it, because nothing is perfect. But we are going to relentlessly chase it, because in the process we will catch excellence. I am not remotely interested in just being good."

Vince Lombardi

Achieve A Synergy Of Team Effort

When a team is working well together there is a synergy of effort that results in the whole being greater than the sum of its parts. You have selected a team with high integrity, positioned them based on their skills, and aligned their efforts. You have listened to the team and considered their input concerning concepts, first principles, issues, policy, and all ideas for improvements. You will now reap the benefits of this synergy in the excellence of the result.

When geese fly in "V" formation, they achieve a reduction in drag, so less effort is required for all behind the leader. The drag reduction of formation flying comes from surfing the wake of the bird ahead. They honk to encourage each other to keep up the pace. With this "V" formation teamwork, they can travel much greater distances then they could going it alone.

" The whole is more than the sum of its parts."

Aristotle

Part 3.
Inspiring An
Innovation Team

The energy, enthusiasm, optimism, and dedication that you, as the leader, bring to the team will be contagious. Thus, the vision will be turned into actions that deliver the results that you expect. Open communications is one of the most important elements in successful teamwork. There can't be a fear of speaking out and telling the truth about an issue or its solution. Good ideas come from above and below, and all are needed.

Hard work must be respected, and many failures may precede a solution. When a milestone is achieved, take the time to celebrate and enjoy the moment.

The team attitude will be—we intend to be the best at what we do, no one can do it better, and there is no challenge we cannot overcome. The team at its best will love the work they do. They can't wait to get to their job and carry the project to the next level. It's exciting to work on what seems impossible to others.

Discussion Points

1. Lead By Example
2. Motivate Your Team
3. Practice Open Communication & Transparency
4. Walk In Your Associates Moccasins
5. Realize That Fear & Innovation Are Incompatible
6. Value Hard Work
7. Give Recognition & Reward At Key Milestones
8. Coach & Mentor Future Leaders
9. End Every Meeting With Action Items Assigned
10. Love The Work

Lead By Example

You must demonstrate your integrity from day one through your actions and behaviors, remembering that initial impressions are most important. Do not say one thing and do another. If you expect people to come in early and stay late, then you need to be the first one in and the last one out. If you want people to treat all levels of individuals with equal courtesy and respect, then you need to do so in your everyday encounters. If you expect action-oriented decision making, then you must demonstrate this at your level, too.

Never break a promise: every promise kept builds trust. When you have an organization built on mutual trust, you don't need energy wasting bureaucracy.

Always adhere to the principles you preach. Every leader needs to "take the point" and show a willingness to understand, support, and endure what the team is enduring.

" An army of principles will penetrate where an army of soldiers cannot;"

Thomas Paine

Motivate Your Team

You must inspire your team to achieve more than they believe is possible. Your presence, your words, and your confidence at the key decisions points will provide this inspiration.

A large part of what motivates innovative people is to be an integral part of an effort to achieve something that has not been done before. When I joined Pratt & Whitney in 1967, I was assigned to work on the engine for the Boeing 747. This was to be the world's largest airplane and would carry people to every corner of the globe. It was an exciting and challenging program. I was impressed when the program's chief design engineer came to my desk, myself just a new hire, and explained the importance of this program to me personally. Nothing could have been more motivational.

Winston Churchill used his passionate speeches, his imposing presence, and his "V" for victory symbol to successfully motivate millions of Britons during the darkest days of WWII. When all looked hopeless, when others recommended surrender, he insisted on making whatever the effort that was required for victory. It was said that a Churchill speech was worth an army. In the powerful motivational quote below, we see Churchill being respectful of the past, realistic in the present, and optimistic toward the future.

"Upon this battle depends the survival of Christian civilization -- The whole fury and might of the enemy must very soon be turned on us -- if we fail -- the whole world will sink into the abyss of a new dark age -- Let us therefore brace ourselves to our duties, and so bear ourselves, that if the British empire lasts for a thousand years men will still say, this was their finest hour."

Sir Winston Churchill

Practice Open Communication & Transparency

You must possess strong communication skills to lead an innovative team. Less formality and an open door policy are recommended. Remove barriers that impede free information flow. Develop your ability to simplify complex issues and state key points clearly so that all may understand them. Seek the suggestions of the entire team.

Be transparent in what you say and what you do. Stealthy language is harmful. Open communication between all team members will lead to each person understanding their role more completely and taking responsibility for the result. Create and operate in an environment of total openness and transparence.

" A further important factor in Apollo's success -- was the complete openness with which it was conducted. From top administrators -- to scientists and engineers --, to production workers and even floor sweepers -- , there was an intense feeling of personal responsibility for the success of our mission to the Moon."

Dr. Werhner Von Braun

Walk In Your Associates Moccasins

You need to be close to your team to appreciate the challenge of their work and to provide guidance and assistance when necessary. You don't want to make decisions that appear good to you but in reality are harmful to team spirit and the desired results.

You can't understand a team's challenges from behind a desk in a well carpeted front office. The most devastating program failures have resulted from isolated program managers making decisions without front line knowledge. It is not enough to receive information from your direct reports on a critical issue. They may be telling you what they think you want to hear. You need to visit the crisis point and talk to the people who are dealing with the challenge head on. Only then can you weigh all the facts and assist in making the right decisions.

Thomas Edison was always visible and available to his team. He would visit every member of his team and share in their problems. He would dream up solutions with them, right at their desk. His personal involvement and encouragement despite many setbacks was an inspiration to each team member. They knew he would not give up, and neither could they.

Don't be an armchair general. Get out on the shop floor yourself and see the real environment first hand.

" You know, farming looks mighty easy when your plow is a pencil and you're a thousand miles from the corn field."

Dwight D. Eisenhower

Realize That Fear & Innovation Are Incompatible

Trust and respect are the keys if you are to create and maintain open communications. You will never hear the truth if you create an environment of fear around you. You will not be forewarned of an impending crisis.

In an atmosphere of fear, questions are not welcome, new ideas are looked upon with suspicion, and people expect you to tell them what to do. They can't take the initiative; they must wait for formal approvals. Opportunities are missed.

When you see a vulture, you worry: you don't innovate. An atmosphere of fear is incompatible with one of innovation.

" Alexander and Caesar, those renown generals received more faithful service, and performed greater actions by means of the love their soldiers bore them, then they could possibly have done, if instead of being -- respected they had been hated and feared by those they commanded."

Benjamin Franklin

Value Hard Work

Solutions are found by long hours spent probing many options to a tough problem. In a classic fable by Aesop, *Mice In Council*, a young mouse comes up with a solution to a stealthy cat—let's tie a bell around the cat's neck he says. All the council agree, a fine idea an old mouse says, but who is going to tie the bell around the cat's neck? It is much easier to have a good idea than it is to persevere, overcome all obstacles, and finally carry it through to a success. Many schemes must be drawn before the correct embodiment of the original idea finally emerges. The more schemes you have looked at, the more confident you will be that you have selected the right one.

When the Wright brothers took their first gilder to Kitty Hawk and tethered it facing into the wind, it did not have the lift to rise as was anticipated. They went back to Ohio, built their own wind tunnel, rewrote the aerodynamic equations of the day, and redesigned their glider accordingly. They took the new glider to Kitty Hawk the next year and it demonstrated the lift as predicted. When they calculated the power to weight ratio for the engine they needed, there was none available, so they designed and built their own.

Nothing worth doing comes easy. Nature does not give up its secrets without a fight. Many test failures, representing years of intense effort, may precede a successful prototype design.

"Success can be achieved only through repeated failure and introspection. In fact, success represents 1% of your work, which results only from the 99% that is called failure."

Soichiro Honda

Give Recognition & Reward
At Key Milestones

Your project plan will have milestones that recognize important steps forward toward the goal. These milestones will involve long hours of hard work, and when achieved, should be celebrated. Each team member should be able to say to themselves "Yes, I played a significant role; we can do this; we will get there; we will find a way."

You need to take a time out and speak to the team about the achievement of this key milestone on the long road to success and its importance to achieving the overall goal. This will build confidence in each team member—that the milestones that lie ahead are also achievable.

The team needs some rest and relaxation. Take a break, celebrate their successes. Give them the recognition and reward they deserve.

" This is not the end. It is not even the beginning of the end. But it is, perhaps, the end of the beginning."

Sir Winston Churchill

Coach & Mentor Future Leaders

Coach and mentor your young team members: they are your future, and they are born with curiosity and adventure in their hearts. Encourage young team members to ask probing questions and to speak to you on the issues they see. Create no aloofness, no command and control culture, but have instead an open and inviting style.

On one new engine program where we were struggling to reduce the product cost, we hired a retired leader in the field of materials engineering as a consultant. He sat down with me and provided many ideas on new materials to use in new ways that would improve the product and reduce cost. He would return monthly to see how I was doing. We made a lot of great progress, thanks to his broad technical expertise and wonderful coaching style. When we discussed the ideas that did not work out, he would always end with "Son, you can only lick so many lions in a day."

Our future leaders don't have the biases that many more experienced people may develop over the years, they are more open to entertain new thoughts. You will find that good ideas come from these meetings where youth and optimism blend with knowledge gained from experience. They are looking to you for direction, advice and guidance. The time you spend with them will pay rich dividends.

"My grandfather once told me that there are two kinds of people: those who do the work and those who take the credit. He told me to try to be in the first group, there was much less competition there."

Indira Gandhi

End Every Meeting With
Action Items Assigned

Everyone concerned with delivering results on schedule has been frustrated by poorly run meetings that drag on forever, with no decisions to show for it. They finally end with everyone leaving with a different opinion of what was said and what to do next. This fault is the biggest time waster and threat to any program.

Every meeting needs to have a leader, a defined purpose, an agenda, a time keeper, and a recorder to take down the action items and document the decisions. We don't want a hundred action items; we want a few powerful items with a commitment to fund them and meaningful due dates. Meetings are not held just to exchange information; meetings are held to put ideas and data on the table and make a decision.

There needs to be strong follow up on the action items assigned at meetings. These action items have a due date and a person who is technically responsible for approving their completion. Team members should leave every meeting aligned, with clear direction, and clearly defined ownership of agreed action items. Not to decide, is to decide. Never leave till tomorrow what you can decide today.

Create a team of action oriented people who are results driven. They will welcome timely decision making, and the appreciation of their recommendations.

"What can be done with care perform today. Dangers unthought of will attend delay."

Benjamin Franklin

40

Love The Work

When the team is truly inspired they get into it 100%. It becomes a labor of love where every day you break new ground, overcome new challenges, and do things that no one else has done before. Cultivate this spirit of adventure in your team. Thomas Edison reflected on his life's efforts by saying that he never had done a day's work, it had all been fun.

One of the leaders I learned the most from had great energy and enthusiasm combined with a deep technical job knowledge that he freely shared. He once told me "I can't believe they pay me to do this job." He loved his job, and it shined through in all his attributes and inspired his team to create innovations that led to an industry changing product.

The team can't wait to begin each day's great adventure.

"Disneyland is a work of love. We didn't go into Disneyland just with the idea of making money."
                                                    Walt Disney

Part 4.
Developing Key Strategies

Leaders with a vision and a motivated team need to develop the strategy and tactics to support that vision and that team. They need to make knowledge based decisions that are guided by first principles. They need to know their competition and not just where they are now, but where they likely will be when the innovative product comes to market.

Leaders tell themselves the truth up front. Hope is not a strategy. They admit to the difficulties of the path that lies ahead and can realistically formulate a plan to overcome them.

Leaders take a results oriented view. They picture themselves standing with the desired result and look back to where they started. In this way, they can correctly foresee the barriers they must cross to achieve the goal. Leaders take prudent risks aimed at value creation, but they don't take foolish risks. Leaders focus on action, speed, and value in decision making.

Discussion Points

1. Tell The Truth Up Front
2. Take A Results View
3. Strive To Deliver The Finest Results
4. Gather New Data To Support Decisions
5. Seek Independent Expert Critique
6. Make Timely Decisions Based On First Principles
7. Take Prudent Risks
8. Don't Take Foolish Risks
9. Value Your Time
10. Know Your Competitor

Tell the Truth Up Front

To solve challenging problems we must analyze the situation and develop a strategy and actions to resolve them. The biggest mistake we can make is to not be truthful about the degree of difficulty we are facing. Admit to the difficulties that lie ahead as early in the project as possible.

Others may resist the difficult task or news you are putting in front of them, preferring to bury their head or turn away, but inaction, or inadequate action, will be much worse in the long run. It will lead to a failure to apply sufficient resources and effort. President Kennedy clearly laid out the risks involved in the Apollo moon landing program right up front.

"We choose to go to the moon in this decade -- because that goal will serve to organize and measure the best of our energies and skills, because that challenge is one we are willing to accept, one we are unwilling to postpone,-- therefore, we set sail on the most hazardous and dangerous and greatest adventure on which man has ever embarked."

John F. Kennedy

Take A Results View

In the pursuit of a great result, we want to correctly forecast the obstacles and the discontinuities we will encounter, or we will face significant delays ahead. We will likely need to establish technology development programs to overcome those barriers and to enable our innovation to mature in a timely way. We may need to hire and train people in these new disciplines. We may need to procure advanced manufacturing tooling to achieve cost targets and deliver a high quality product.

Imagine achieving the desired result, then look back to where your efforts began. You would then see all the bridges you need to cross and all the barriers you need to overcome en route to your goal.

"You always start with a fantasy. Part of the fantasy technique is to visualized something as perfect. Then with experiments you work your way back from fantasy to reality, hacking away at the components."

Edwin H. Land

Strive To Deliver The Finest Results

Well done is always better than well said. The number of summary slides it takes to present the status of a project is inversely proportional to the quality of the result. A successful project can be summarized in a few short slides, but a failure will require a much longer explanation and a recovery plan.

You may be called upon to solve a difficult challenge in an innovative project that may have gotten off to a bad start. This has happen to me many times in my career. You will enter a situation of long drawn out meetings, with many slides defining bad results, and with very unhappy people demanding more meetings. You need to put your solution team together, insist on time away from information sharing meetings, find the root cause of the problem, and put your solution on the table. The key is to select the right concept based on first principles, and then to get a prototype made to prove the point. When the prototype is successful, only a few slides and a short meeting will be necessary to share the good news.

This is why It is important to realize that the concept phase of a project is the most critical, and to put in that extra effort up front that will pay big dividends downstream. Too often a project gets off to a bad start— under staffed, under funded, and late relative to the due date. It's worth the effort to do it right the first time and to bring in the desired result on time and on budget.

"It takes less time to do a thing right then it does to explain why you did it wrong"

Henry Wadsworth Longfellow

Gather New Data To Support Decisions

We may find that existing data is not sufficient to advance our concept. We cannot resolve many difficult problems without digging in, doing a root-cause analysis, and spending the appropriate time and manpower to reach a thorough understanding. Quick decisions that are made without this necessary information can lead to disaster. You can't solve a problem at the same level of knowledge and with the same data with which it was created.

Consult with experts in the field and do your own research in the areas vital to the innovation. The Wright brothers built their own wind tunnel and designed their own airfoils to determine the correct equations for lift. This is the norm when you are on the leading edge of the technology. Gather new information to resolve a tough problem. Make data based decisions.

"Those who fall in love with practice without science are like a sailor who enters a ship without a helm or a compass, and who never can be certain whither he is going."

Leonardo da Vinci

Seek Independent Expert Critique

You may need to team with an individual or company that has the expertise in an engineering or manufacturing area vital to your innovation. Employing an expert in an area that is new to you and your team can make the difference in accomplishing the project goal. Bringing in a world-class expert to share his or her experience and knowledge can add that little extra lift to get a project soaring. But in the end, your team must still make the correct choices, and assume the responsibility for all decisions.

On one component job I led, requiring a high strength low cost material, we brought in an expert that taught materials at the local university. He had an in-depth knowledge of a material that was new to us. He knew the mines from which the ore was extracted, the mills that processed the ore, the heat treatment options that we could apply, and the results that we could expect. Once convinced of the value of the new material, we needed to commit resources to develop property data for the engineers to use in the design of the parts. This material turned out to be vital to the achievement of the component goals, and we could not have brought it home without this consultant.

Bring in independent experts and combine their new information with the materials you have mined yourself, and do all your homework. When a good consultant is present, the client solves the problem, and in the end the success is yours to enjoy.

"A genius is often merely a talented person who has done all of his or her homework."

Thomas Edison

Make Timely Decisions Based On First Principles

We have gathered new information, we have consulted the experts, and now we must make decisions. These decisions must also be aligned with first principles. First principles can be scientific, financial, moral, and in some cases, they can be all three. They are truths that will guide us while we combine art and science into an innovative product or service that improves the life experience of our customers.

We will be building from the first principles established by the leaders and innovators that came before us. Know and respect their work so that you might then advance the state of the art. Edison read every book and article on the subject of his invention. He started where the last person left off. His thought processes depended on this keen knowledge of the basic principles of electricity, magnetism, materials properties, acoustics, and mechanics. If I were asked to design an aircraft engine with the lowest fuel consumption, I know that the basic principles of engine performance require me to provide the highest cycle and propulsive efficiency. All my innovative concepts must be guided by this reality.

Isaac Newton was the first scientist to understand and correctly explain the force of gravity and the motion of the planets around the sun. Newton's three laws of motion became the standard physics of his day. He clearly recognized that his breakthrough thinking was built on the principles and work of many who came before him.

"If I have seen further it is by standing on the shoulders of giants."

Sir Isaac Newton

Take Prudent Risks

Have the confidence and courage to take a risk. There is no progress made without prudent risk taking. You may not walk on water, but your experience, judgment, and intuition will guide you through the challenge.

Create a risk management plan that anticipates problem areas based on the new technologies being added. Develop subsystem rigs and prototypes where necessary to reinforce technical understanding. Work technology readiness into the engineering, manufacturing, and supplier areas. Add systems engineering strength, if you are partnering out critical subsystems.

You may need to cross thin ice on the road to a product break through: courage is a necessary attribute.

"You gain strength courage and confidence by every experience in which you really stop to look fear in the face.-- you must do the things you think you can not do."

Eleanor Roosevelt

Don't Take Foolish Risks

Having the courage to take risk is a required attribute to lead a team in innovating a breakthrough product. No great advances were made without risk, but there is no need to take foolish risk.

Are we improving an existing product that is soon to be made obsolete? Are we investing large sums in a brand new product with just a marginal advantage over existing products? Are we counting on a new technology without having invested in bringing it home? Are we partnering out a critical part of the work without adequate systems engineering interface definition?

Balance risk and reward. Smart risk taking means not making foolish choices. Be bold, but be smart. Obey first principles. There is nothing to be gained by deliberately perching on a high-power line.

"I think that there is only one quality worse than hardness of heart and that is softness of head."

Theodore Roosevelt

Value Your Time

Time, once lost, can never be recaptured. When time is highly valued, it becomes the enabler of those extra activities that lead to the acquisition of wisdom and knowledge. When I was managing my time efficiently, I knew it because I had time to think about new innovative processes and product solutions.

The biggest time waster is too many "information only" meetings. Meetings need to be held to make decisions. You need to decide not to attend all the meetings you are invited to. As difficult as that may seem, it was a key element in the successful completion of many of my assignments. I once told a program manager that I could either attend all of his meetings or deliver a great product. He wisely chose the product, and success was assured.

Prioritizing email is another key element. Emails need to state in their first paragraph what they are about and what they conclude. I was taught to tell them what you are going to tell them, and then tell them what you told them, as a matter of course. You can set this up with your direct reports. Then you can quickly decide to read them in depth, or pass them on to someone else.

Organize your day around your own body rhythms. Only you know if you are more creative in the morning and more analytical in the afternoon. Limit your time spent on bureaucracy, and spend your time developing people and planning and building creative processes and products.

"Dost thou love life? Then do not squander time, for that's the stuff life is made of."

Benjamin Franklin

Know Your Competitor

Respect and study the competition to recognize their strengths and weaknesses. The end goal is world leadership, and you need a plan to exceed their best efforts in every area of customer satisfaction.

Plan to best your competition at the three levels of product value. The system you offer should provide simplicity of use in terms of both hardware and software, and it should be superior in overall value. The components that comprise the system should offer the next level of technological innovation— something to excite the customers that they were not expecting. The individual parts should be designed for manufacturability, reliability, and low cost.

You must benchmark your competition and offer more market value, or they will swoop down and surprise you with a market changing product.

" I have been up against tough competition all my life. I wouldn't know how to get along without it."

Walt Disney

Part 5.
Elements Of An Innovative Product

An innovative product concept evolves from a vision of an improved future state. That product can be revolutionary and create its own market. The Wright Flyer and the Sikorsky helicopter are examples of concepts that created new industries. An innovative product can be evolutionary, and meet a known customer need. The electric powered cars that are now gaining traction in the auto market are meeting a known customer need for personal transportation with reduced air pollution.

The new product must provide improved value versus competing existing products. Value is a simple equation of the functional experience provided divided by the price. Value can be judged by considering the provided technology, quality, availability, and service versus the price. When a product is fully optimized for maximum value, all of its components are synergistically combined to optimize the ownership experience. Simplicity and elegance of design execution will reduce cost and weight while improving reliability and owner loyalty.

<u>Discussion Points</u>

1. Creates An Industry
2. Solves A Known Customer Need
3. Provides A New User Experience
4. Provides A Better Mouse Trap
5. Recognizes The Interconnectivity Of All Things
6. Recognizes The Synergy Of Product Components
7. Features A Simple And Elegant Product Design
8. Features A Breakthrough Concept
9. Is Demonstrated By A Prototype
10. Has 90% Of Its Value Set By The Concept Choice

Creates An Industry

It was just over one hundred years ago that the Wright brothers developed and flew the first controllable aircraft for 57 seconds covering 852 feet. From that humble beginning, we evolved to today's advanced aviation industry where we can fly non-stop to almost any point on the globe.

Igor Sikorsky invented the first successful vertical takeoff aircraft, the helicopter. His company still thrives today, and so does the industry he founded. The machine could take off and hover like a humming bird and save people's lives.

" If a man is in need of a rescue, an airplane can come in and throw flowers on him, and that's about all. But a direct lift aircraft can come in and save his life." -- "The helicopter approaches closer than any other vehicle to the fulfillment of man's ancient dream of the flying horse and the magic carpet."

Igor Sikorsky

Solves A Known Customer Need

Your innovation may be addressing a known customer need. Thomas Edison addressed the real need for clean, safe, and efficient lighting by creating the electric light bulb and all the systems supporting equipment to light lower Manhattan.

Henry Ford met the American family's need for affordable transportation. He did not invent the first automobile, but he created and built a simple car that could be mass produced; a car that could run on available fuel and was drivable on the unimproved roads of the day—the famous Model T.

The creation of the Boeing 747 airliner addressed the need for long range air transportation at lower ticket prices and with much quieter and more fuel efficient engines. This jumbo aircraft could fly non-stop from New York to Tokyo at a level of comfort and at a price not possible before.

The need to have less pollution in large cities and improve gas mileage is being addressed today by revolutionary advances in hybrid and electric cars. New companies, such as Tesla, have been founded to bring this technology to market. They have provided the customer with all electric cars with more than 200 miles range.

Customers face a daunting problem and are in need of a solution: you will provide it.

"If you sense a deep human need, then you go back to all the basic science. If there is some(thing) missing, then you try and do more basic science and applied science till you get it. So you make the system to fulfill that need --"

Edwin H. Land

Provides A New User Experience

We have discussed innovations that create a new industry and innovations that meet a known customer need. There are also innovations that improve customer's lives beyond their current needs and expectations. The customer doesn't always know all that is possible. This is especially true when one considers the rapid advances in technology in so many overlapping fields. There is an opportunity to combine these new technologies to create a new user experience

The iPhone is an example of a product that took the cellular phone to a level beyond what customers might have thought they needed. It created a new market segment: the smart phone. You must now anticipate customer needs and create a new user experience that does not exist in the market today. This opportunity can be an evolutionary or disruptive change that makes the competition's products pale in comparison. My daily newspaper was many times delivered wet or late or not at all. The solution was a digital subscription and an iPad. That worked out so well that I switched my magazine subscriptions to digital also. They always arrive dry and on time and I can increase the print size when necessary—a great user experience.

An innovation's success is determined by the customer. Look at the lines that form, sometimes days in advance, outside an Apple store when they offer a new product. The user experience defines a successful innovation better than any specifications can do.

"It's really hard to design products by focus groups. A lot of times people don't know what they want until you show it to them."

Steve Jobs

Provides A Better Mouse Trap

If our goal is to provide a new product that will dominate the competition, then we must always keep in mind the five rights of the customer: the right technology, the right quality, the right service, the right timing, and the right price. These are the elements of value, and each one must be addressed if we are to outpace the competition with our innovation.

We need to select advanced but proven technology that is ready to go into production. This will provide our product with unique features that yield a new user experience. If we strive for simplicity in our concept, we will have an edge in achieving the highest level of quality— namely, fewer components with fewer parts and with features that are producible by advanced manufacturing methods. Customer service is what creates brand loyalty. No one wants to hear the recorded phone message "your call is very important to us" while you wait forever to speak to a service representative. Timing your entry into the market is a matter of not being too early, before the technology is reliable, yet being bold enough not to wait for someone else to prove the concept will sell.

The market place will set the price, so carefully and respectfully benchmark the competition. This will cause you to set tougher goals that will put your innovation far ahead of the pack. If the concept selected is the right one, and the quality is such that its value far exceeds that of the competition, people will beat a path to your door.

"If a man can write a better book, or preach a better sermon, or build a better mouse trap than his neighbor, though he builds his home in the woods, the world will make a beaten path to his door."

Ralph Waldo Emerson

Recognizes The Interconnectivity Of All Things

Recognizing how an innovation will alter its planned environment, and how it will harmonize with current products and customer needs, is a key to the product's success. Be a systems-level thinker, see the big picture. Understand how your innovation changes that picture.

Einstein saw the universe as an understandable and interconnected system. His theories of special and general relativity changed our perception of space and time itself. Today we know that there are planets in orbit around nearby stars by the small wobble they cause in the orbit of those stars. Our perception of the universe has changed. We now know most stars have planets, some in the habitable zone. Below, Leonardo shares an Einstein type thought 400 years before Einstein.

" The earth is moved from its position by the weight of a tiny bird resting upon it."

Leonardo da Vinci

Recognizes The Synergy Of Product Components

The correct systems solution will be a synergy of current and advanced technology that will achieve the project goals at minimum risk. It will represent a combination of art and science and a balance of logic and imagination. Systems integration involves understanding both the functions of the individual components, and how to combine them in a fully optimized system.

When an airplane is designed, it is not a wing, a tail, a fuselage, and engine designed independently, but it is a fully integrated dependent system. Flying requires the perfect integration of all the bodies components. Each component is designed, or evolved in the case of birds, to optimize the system as a whole. Long slender wings for high lift with low drag, hollow bones and feathers for weight reduction and eye sight capable at long distances.

" All parts of the system must be constructed with reference to all other parts, since in one sense, all the parts form one machine."

Thomas Edison

Features A Simple And Elegant Product Design

Hugely successful products like the Apple iPhone & iPad are perfect examples of technology used to simplify the product and maximize customer value. The product should be so intuitive and simple to operate that you don't need a user's manual.

The product with the lowest complexity normally has the lightest weight, lowest cost, and best reliability. Design is an art as well as a science, and it is the perfect integration of these two disciplines that we seek in our product.

A bird has every component of its body aligned to perform its intended function, and combined in a simple and elegant solution to permit the miracle of flight.

"When you first start off trying to solve a problem, the first solutions you come with are very complex -- But if you keeping going and live with the problem and peel more layers of the onion off, you can often times arrive at some very elegant and simple solutions."

Steve Jobs

Features A Breakthrough Concept

Breakthrough or disruptive product concepts can make existing technology obsolete overnight. They can create new industries and effectively wipe out older ones. Examples are: the iPhone establishing the smart phone market, iPod technology replacing CDs, electronic watches replacing gear and spring watches, electronic calculators replacing slide rules, and digital cameras replacing film cameras. In these cases, an existing industry either disappeared, or was relegated to a secondary player by a new technology product whose value far exceeded the existing product.

When digital cameras arrived some people did not realize their potential. But a look at first principles would tell you straight away that the light collecting CCD chip they were based on was destined to far exceed the capabilities of film. They ushered in the wonderful era of the digital dark room for all of us to enjoy. They permitted instant review of pictures taken. Some film makers adapted early and got into digital, but others waited too long and lost out.

Breakthrough products offer a level of utility and value that the customer has not experienced before. The developers of these products have persevered to overcome barriers that others saw as insurmountable. They searched for answers to the toughest problems and endured many hardships until they found them.

There will be a breakthrough in every industry including our own, our job is to find it.

"There is always a way to do it better - find it."

Thomas Edison

Is Demonstrated By A Prototype

Prototypes are a proof of concept. They can be extremely valuable in convincing both backers and potential customers to support your innovation. They can also provide significant technical learning to advance the product design. The prototype of a concept is typically a non-production embodiment of the concept that can be built quickly and at much lower cost than a production product.

In the gas turbine engine world, a company can prototype a new engine concept by taking components that are not part of the innovation from an existing engine, and then combining them with the breakthrough component concept. In this way, only the newly advanced components need to be designed and procured. The prototype engine is then built-up with this combination of new and existing technology components. This can be very effective in demonstrating parameters such as reduced fuel consumption or noise to potential customers.

Today there is a new 3D printer industry that is maturing quickly. This technology allows innovators to create a computer 3D model of their innovation's parts and then produce them quickly without the time and cost of procuring tooling and fixtures. It has the additional advantage that many parts that would have had to be made individually can now be combined into one. The inevitable modifications to the concept can be quickly produced and demonstrated. Take advantage of 3D prototyping and set up an innovation lab now. Show the customers what your innovation can do for them.

"I see a worthwhile need to be met and I make trial after trial until it comes."

Thomas Edison

Has 90% Of Its Value Set By The Concept Choice

The concept phase of a program is the most important since it can determine 90% of the value of the final product. The number-one cause of missed targets is failure to provide a concept that inherently makes the targets. Insist on seeing a concept that makes the targets, and ask what criteria may need to be modified to make this concept viable.

We tend to under staff the concept phase and not provide sufficient time to evaluate all the options. Rushing the wrong product to market can cost you billions of dollars. You need to study the options carefully and then select the right concept based on functionality, simplicity, and total value. This Red-Tailed Hawk represents optimized attributes yielding high value in a flight born predator.

"When we consider a project, we really study it - not just the surface idea, but everything about it. And when we go into that new project, we believe in it all the way. We have confidence in our ability to do it right. And we work hard to do the best possible job."

Walt Disney

Part 6.
Delivering The Innovative Product

Delivering innovative change involves not only the vision, the team, the strategies, and the product itself, but it also involves being a constant advocate for innovation and change in the face of resistance that will certainly come. Resistance generally takes three forms: technical issues, financial issues, and roadblocks placed by people. These three issues are often interrelated. A program that falls behind schedule due to technical issues will soon have financial issues that will cause some former supporters to press for cancellation.

The Wright brothers faced a daunting technical issue when their glider did not have the lift forces predicted. Thomas Edison faced stiff resistance from the gas lighting industry when he proposed providing electric lighting for lower Manhattan. Walt Disney faced a huge challenge to raise the money to create Disneyland. The bolder the innovation, the more resistance to be faced and overcome.

People related issues are perhaps the most difficult because many times their root cause is hidden below the surface of their stated concern. There are those whose vested interests would be adversely effected; there are those who are comfortable with the status quo, and there are those who just fight any change.

With excellent strategy and tactics and planning and preparation we can deal with the resistances we will face and avoid a crisis situation. But, there will be times when things go wrong and people will show up at your desk insisting you must turn back. A crisis is an unplanned event—that's what makes it a crisis. Your confidence and courage will be tested along with your leadership skills.

Discussion Points

1. Step Out Of Your Comfort Zone
2. Be A Force For Positive Change
3. Confront The Unreasonable Critic
4. Be Prepared To Cross Difficult Roads
5. Monitor Progress - Don't Accept Smiles
6. Recognize A Key Issue When Others Do Not
7. Address A Problem Before It's Too Late To Fix
8. Take A leadership Role In A Crisis
9. Advocate For Continuous Innovation
10. Attitude -Program Failure Can Not Be An Option

Step Out Of Your Comfort Zone

We need to experiment with new ideas and this will lead to some risk and discomfort. Expertise in new disciplines may be required, causing us to hire new people in engineering and manufacturing. A shift in the technical leadership and research investment of the company may be called for. Partnerships with leading companies in required technology areas may be appropriate.

Too many times we ask for big improvements in product parameters but are too risk adverse to approve a radical configuration that will deliver the goods. If the new concept configuration looks essentially like the last one, why do we believe it will achieve the new parameters? A game-changing product will require a game-changing concept.

Progress is not made by staying in our comfort zones.

" I have little patience with scientists who take a board of wood, look for the thinnest part, and drill a great number of holes when the drilling is easy."

Albert Einstein

Be A Force For Positive Change

Question the customer value of the products and processes that you inherit. You will see the need for improvement or, perhaps, even a need for a major change. To define future innovations you need to visit your customers, technologists, and design teams.

Visit your customers, evaluate their short and long-term needs and problems and determine how you can help to resolve them. How can you help them today, tomorrow, a year from now? Dig deep— don't be superficial. Spend the time to talk to a broad cross section of their leadership.

Visit your technologists, to find out what new technologies are already in the works, and what they would like to do if they had more resources. Focus them on how these technologies translate into a game-changing product. Share with them the summary of customer needs and expectations.

Visit your team members, discuss the customer requirements, the technologies you have in work, and leave them with ideas and encouragement. Focus them on a market-changing innovation. Plan to design a breakthrough product. Cast a big shadow. Have the courage to set lofty goals for this innovative product. Take the financial risk and step forward and commit the new innovative product to production in time to best the competition.

"We're gambling on our vision, and we would rather do that than make "me too" products. Let some other companies do that. For us, it's always the next dream."

Steve Jobs

Confront The Unreasonable Critic

People who don't want to change, who are protecting their turf, who want to avoid R&D costs, who are satisfied to lay back and make a profit on existing products, will resist and criticize a new idea. This is to be expected.

Question the critics and ask them for their proposals. What are their plans for the future of the business? How do they propose to confront the competition? Face their issues head-on and see if you can formulate a win-win proposal.

You may be up against an inept and unreasonable critic, a "turkey." The critics are out there, be prepared to face them.

"It is not the critic that counts, not the man who points out how the strong man stumbles or where the doer of deeds could have done them better. The credit belongs to the man who is actually in the arena; -- who strives valiantly: who errs -- but who actually does strive to do the deeds."

Theodore Roosevelt

Be Prepared To Cross Difficult Roads

There will be obstacles to overcome on the path to success of any important innovation. A diligent effort to anticipate and prepare for these problem areas upfront will pay big rewards downstream. This is where the resolve of the leader will be put to the test. These obstacles can be financial, technological, or related to product metrics such as weight, cost, performance, durability, and many others. If you have performed a good risk analysis upfront, you will have funded alternate paths and be prepared to overcome most of these issues. Still, there will be unplanned issues that become a crisis if not addressed vigorously and promptly.

The new technologies you are introducing are an area of obvious risk. You need to understand the risk of each technology relative to the state of the art. More risk requires more upfront investment in time and resources. You might be working 50 technologies, but it is not necessary or likely that they all will bear fruit. You need to have fall back positions planned in the event that returns are not realized. You need to monitor their progress, be prepared to assist in overcoming issues, or move to the backup position. Backup plans should not be fluff. When they are required they must be real and ready to go.

Recognize each barrier and its risks, choose the time and place to overcome it, cross when you are ready. Minimize crises by addressing issues decisively. Be prepared for a crisis, but never give up the vision.

"Obstacles cannot crush me. Every obstacle yields to stern resolve."

Leonardo da Vinci

Monitor Progress - Don't Accept Smiles

Monitoring progress is part of a leaders job. Although some team members may prefer not to be transparent on issues they face. You must insist on transparency, or they will show up and tell you all is lost when it is too late to fix. This is one of many areas where an environment of open communications is so important. Team members need to feel free to report problems, and need to have confidence that you will help in the resolution and not attack them personally. Deal directly and promptly with the issues and their resolution.

On one of a number of propulsion system projects I was responsible for, the team was not transparent. They were reporting that things were going well until the team leader came to me at the last minute with such a significant problem that it would have caused us to miss the delivery date. This crisis could have easily been avoided if the problems had been reported earlier and the team had given the senior leaders a chance to help with the solution. It took a major effort to recover. With the addition of manpower, manufacturing resources, and new leadership it was still possible to resolve the issues and deliver the new innovative product to the customer on time. We learned that leadership training needs to emphasis transparency and open communications.

A healthy confrontation on the key issues may be required, but should never deteriorate into a shouting match. Demand progress reports and ask probing questions while all the while maintaining your civility. There will be cases however, where new leadership is required.

"Speak softly and carry a big stick; you will go far."

Theodore Roosevelt

Recognize A Key Issue
When Others Do Not

Raising an alert and making people aware of a problem is never well received at first notice but can save the day in the long run. Many times peoples first instinct is to "kill the messenger." You must work through this difficult phase to deliver the required message.

Always offer a solution to a problem, even if it represents a difficult path. The hardship that an early solution imposes will be small compared to the hardships faced later if the problem is not addressed. Remain calm in the face of criticism and anger and keep redirecting the conversation to address the issue and not the persons involved.

A problem cannot be resolved until it is identified. The longer it festers, the harder it will be to solve. Give the roar—alert the team!

"People kindly said that I inspired the nation. It was the nation -- that had the lion heart. I had the luck to be called upon to give the roar."

Sir Winston Churchill

Address A Problem Before It's Too Late To Fix

Tell yourself the truth upfront and that will allow you to fix a small problem before it becomes a big problem. Look around the world today and you will find that the main cause of unsolved problems is an unwillingness to admit that there is a problem. Problems are like tooth aches: they don't get better on their own. Hope is not a strategy; we cannot wish a problem away.

When a design is on paper, it is a lot easier and less costly to fix then when it is in hardware. After you have spent hundreds of millions of dollars procuring hardware, it is difficult to admit that you have chosen the wrong concept, and much of the money spent to date will be wasted. There is a tendency to believe that a small change will bring success, even when the facts say otherwise.

I have seen engine concepts defined that did not make the key target parameters. Charts were put in place to show that changes to the configuration over time would result in closing the gaps. The charts, however, were full of wishful thinking, and the changes that they did propose were not actually funded. What I would call fluff. The sooner you admit that a significant change is required, the better off you will be.

Studying something to death is not the answer. When a big tree is leaning precariously toward you, don't wait for it to fall. When the situation demands a response, inaction is not the answer.

"Be ready to revise any system, scrap any method, abandon any theory, if the success of the job requires it."

Henry Ford

Take A Leadership Role In A Crisis

You have done all you can to avoid a crisis, but they can still happen. A crisis takes us to an unplanned area—that's what makes it a crisis. The attributes of the leader are tested in a crisis. Self-confidence is built up with years of experience leading teams through crisis situations.

Break an apparently daunting problem into solvable pieces. Assign a strong leader to each of these pieces. Give them the resources and decision making authority to advance to the solution. Review their progress regularly, and provide additional support when necessary. Your personal involvement and encouragement will make a difference.

Don't accept chaos. Remain confident and restore order through calm, innovative, and courageous decision making.

"Any featherhead can have confidence in times off victory, but the test is to have faith when things are going wrong."

Sir Winston Churchill

Advocate For Continuous Innovation

You should constantly hire creative and disruptive thinkers and establish an environment and culture that supports breakthrough thinking. This is important not just in delivering the current product in development, but for all future products. Every presentation and discussion provides an opportunity to drive innovation and create and maintain an innovative culture. It's not only about continuous improvement, six sigma and standard work, innovation will play a bigger role in your future than any of these.

Support both evolutionary and disruptive change. You need to be constantly working on incremental improvements to your current products that will represent your new standard work, while at the same time, you strategize and plan for major disruptive changes.

I believe a large company should have a chief innovation officer in the same way it has a chief financial officer. You need a person who is on top of the technologies that are important in your industry and who can speak in defense of the technology investments that are required but are too often under critical review. This person could open the door for creative people to present their ideas at the highest decision making level.

Talk about imagination, creativity, bold new products, and the positive changes they will bring. Make it part of your daily discussions with every team member.

"Since new developments are the products of a creative mind, we must therefore stimulate and encourage that type of mind in every way possible."

George Washington Carver

Attitude - Program Failure Can Not Be An Option

There will be times of crisis after setbacks during difficult projects when people insist that you turn back. No one wins every battle; you will be knocked down, perhaps many times. Your future vision, plans, and strategies will be tested. Do not cancel the program and accept failure. The key to success is to bounce back and make the big changes required to resolve the crisis without delay.

The crisis will be a true test of your leadership skills. You will look back on this crisis as a necessary learning experience. Have confidence—your tenacity will carry the day. Don't turn back; instead, face and resolve the issues now. The winter spent at Valley Forge was the great crisis of the American Revolution where George Washington's leadership prevailed.

"These are the times that try men's souls, in this crisis the summer soldier and the sunshine patriot will shrink from the service of their country."

Thomas Paine

Part 7.
Attributes That Enable A Leader

We have discussed the dream and vision, the formation of a team, the development of strategies, and the elements and delivery of an innovative change. To successfully navigate this path, there are essential attributes that leaders must have, develop, and improve. These attributes will enable the actions and behaviors that will deliver the desired results..

Leaders are systems-level thinkers who see the big picture. They are self-confident and courageous enough to make bold decisions and defend them with first principles and logic. They are not intimated by doubters and naysayers. They seek and capture opportunities that others may miss. They communicate openly and clearly without deception.

They have earned the respect of all through their ability and integrity.

Discussion Points

1. Systems Level Thinker
2. Self-Confident & Decisive
3. Committed To Excellence
4. Courageous & Bold
5. Optimistic & Resourceful
6. Diligent & Persistent
7, Opportunistic
8. Vigilant
9. Excellent Communicator
10. Respected By All - Integrity

Systems Level Thinker

Leaders are systems level thinkers who see the big picture and think globally. While focusing on the important details of an issue, they never lose sight of the systems level goals of the program and the end product value they deliver to the world's customers.

Leonardo da Vinci, Thomas Edison, and Albert Einstein were systems-level thinkers. Leonardo defined systems-level concepts for moving water, for flying, and for the human body. Edison defined a fully integrated system of light bulbs, generators, cables, outlets, and switches, that worked harmoniously together. Einstein, with his theories of relativity, proved that the universe itself was an understandable system. For the first time man could understand how the sun could shine for billions of years and how light could be bent by gravity. Be a systems-level thinker.

"A human being is a part of the whole, called by us "The Universe," a part limited in time and space. Our task must be to free ourselves -- by widening our circle of compassion to embrace all living creatures and the whole of nature in its beauty."

Albert Einstein

Self-Confident & Decisive

Welcome the start of each new day. Each day will bring challenges and opportunities. When the sun rises we need to be alert, optimistic, trusting of our intuition, and prepared to take on the events of the day. Be decisive, there are decisions that must be made today, after you carefully weigh all the information and team recommendations.

You will attend meetings where opposing ideas are put on the table and the group is divided into two or more factions. You need to be able to weigh the facts, summarize the opportunities and challenges, and provide a straight forward solution that everyone can understand. Confident decision making is what keeps projects on schedule and within budget.

Self-confidence does not mean arrogance. We appreciate and welcome the suggestions of those trusted experts around us. Some experts will speak up and tell you and the team what they think and provide recommendations. Others are quiet, and you need to prod them or you will miss their vital observations. Always make use of all of your resources. Don't fear a contrary opinion, we don't want a team of "yes men," we need everyone's analysis.

Every day is an opportunity to gain new insight and knowledge to advance our dreams. Believe in yourself and your team and be ready to capture those daily opportunities.

"You have to trust in something -- your gut, destiny, life, karma, whatever. This approach has never let me down, and it has made all the difference in my life."

Steve Jobs

Committed To Excellence

Be passionate towards the program goals and be results driven, but also strive to be compassionate towards the members of your team from whom you are requiring extra effort. Be committed to achieving excellence in both of these attributes, which are truly interwoven.

Strive to be the best in the world at what you do and instill this trait in your team members. Tackle those opportunities that you and your team are uniquely qualified to do. The quality of your life will be determined by your commitment to excellence.

Excellence requires a high level of intensity and focus that you can see in the eyes and posturing of this Green Heron.

"Excellence is never an accident. It is always the result of high intention, sincere effort, and intelligent execution, it represents the wise choice of many alternatives - choice, not chance, determines your destiny."

Aristotle

Courageous & Bold

The most worthwhile things in life are the most difficult to achieve. That is the very reason to take them on. They are the source of experience and learning that will serve us well into the future. They unleash our latent creativity. They give us the confidence to make the next great leap forward.

President Kennedy proposed in 1961 that the United States take on the task within the decade of landing a man on the moon and bringing him back safely to Earth. This was a courageous proposition that involved overcoming huge obstacles. With innovations not yet on the table, many believed that the timeframe was impossible. The NASA team, which brilliantly led the effort, knew that they were facing the greatest challenge ever set upon any team. They needed to make bold and timely decisions daily to keep the schedule. The Apollo program spawned major advancements in technologies, such as the integrated circuit and systems management software, that positively affected all our lives today.

Volunteer for the most difficult jobs, make the bold changes that will assure success, stick with it to the end. Never quit before finishing. Make that extra effort to launch yourself toward a difficult goal or result.

==

"If I were to say to my fellow citizens, that we shall send to the moon -- a giant rocket almost 300 feet tall -- made of new metal alloys, some of which have not yet been invented, -- fitted together with a precision better than the finest watch, -- and then return it safely to earth, -- and do it first before this decade is out -- then we must be bold ."

John F. Kennedy

Optimistic & Resourceful

Optimism is contagious: it is a force multiplier. It leads us and those around us to accomplish things that others think impossible. Many failures may precede a success; we should see each as a lesson that teaches us how to take the next step forward.

Einstein talked about having a hundred ideas and finding ninety- nine of them to be wrong until, at long last, light dawned upon him revealing a breakthrough theory. When he predicted, in the general theory of relativity, that light would be bent by a gravitational field, many physicists were skeptical. He defended his theory for years until British scientists were able to observe this phenomena in the bending of star light during an eclipse of the sun. After this, Einstein's name was known in every household.

Thomas Edison would divide a difficult problem into solvable pieces and attack each piece with a matrix of all available resource options. He had his assistants search the world for a suitable material for the filament of his electric light. One solution was the carbonized fibers of a tree from a Japanese forest. When, despite the best efforts of many people, the filament would not last, he realized a vacuum would solve the problem. He then set out to create a vacuum based bulb. He never gave up, expending all of his resources until a solution was found. We must be resourceful and propose new theories and try new approaches until the objective is in hand.

"I speak without exaggeration when I say I have constructed 3,000 different theories in connection with the electric light, -- Yet only in two cases did my experiments prove the truth of my theory."

Thomas Edison

Diligent & Persistent

Your energy and enthusiasm will spread to your team and carry it through the challenges that lie ahead. Your persistence and tenacity in support of your vision will overcome all obstacles.

When you're not getting the right answer to a question, ask it again from a new perspective. When your experiment does not deliver the expected result, try it again with revised parameters—trick mother nature into revealing her secrets through intelligence, toughness, and persistence.

When the Wright Brothers first glider would not take off as they had expected, they went back to their Ohio bike shop, found the root cause, and changed their wing design accordingly.

A wet Cormorant will bound many times on the surface of the water before it achieves flight. The more diligence you apply, the harder you try; the more effort you put in, the harder it is to quit.

"Diligence is the mother of good luck."

Benjamin Franklin

Opportunistic

A challenge may be disguised as a problem on the surface, but in reality be a growth opportunity. You may be offered a transfer to another department or division that faces a major issue. This is an opportunity for growth, take it. The harder the job, the more you learn and the more confidence you will have for the future. This difficult job may be accompanied by a new and demanding boss. Again, an opportunity to grow and learn from what may well be a different leadership style.

Liquid rubber accidentally spilling on a hot stove led Charles Goodyear to discover the vulcanization process for durable tires. You have to be diligent in trying options, but you also need to be observant enough to recognize and capture an opportunity.

A culture jar containing bacteria, accidentally contaminated with a fungus, led Alexander Fleming to discover penicillin. It took an observant eye, a keen insight into its significance, and many hours of hard work, to turn what might have been an easily overlooked contamination issue, into a great discovery that would save many lives.

Opportunities show up in unexpected places and at unexpected times. They may involve you dropping what you are currently doing, or a completely changing the direction of a project. Be on the alert for opportunities—they may only knock once.

" Opportunity is missed by most people because it is dressed in overalls and looks like work."

Thomas Edison

Vigilant

Be vigilant and alert to particulars that may require a change in your direction and plans. The best plan is one that is continuously improved with new details and knowledge.

Businesses that rented DVD movies were not always vigilant to the new technology of streaming entertainment. This cost them most of the market and drove many out of business. Companies that had dominated the cellular phone market were not all vigilant to the introduction of smart phones. They soon found themselves in deep technical and financial trouble.

This is a highly competitive world where information is available almost instantaneously, and may require your immediate attention and a strong follow-up. Be alert, stand above the crowd, maintain a sharp eye on your competitors, and be prepared to respond.

"The price of liberty is eternal vigilance."

Thomas Jefferson

Excellent Communicator

Communication is the key to accomplishing the goal. You must clearly share your vision, strategy, and tactics with the team and listen carefully to their concerns and recommendations. Emphasize a policy of no surprises. We need to share information in a timely manner so that corrections in course are possible.

Good ideas are welcome from above and below in an open environment. Develop a coaching style of information sharing that will encourage two way communication. Experience has shown that some of the finest ideas come from unexpected sources that are revealed through this open door environment. During one of the most challenging gas turbine engine projects I led, my engineering staff traveled to the manufacturing plant responsible for making the majority of our parts. The engineers were explaining one of the bigger challenges on the rotor design when a manufacturing engineer stood up and proposed a revolutionary concept that led to the ultimate solution. It was not his job, and if this had been a one-way communication by engineering, we would still be searching for the answer. Communication is a two-way street.

When addressing a large group, or where there is not opportunity for effective two-way communication, speak economically with power and emotion using words that everyone can understand. Your body language should reflect your words and emotions.

"Victory at all costs, victory in spite of all terror, victory however long and hard the road might be; for without victory there is no survival."

Sir Winston Churchill

Respected By All-Integrity

Respect is earned by the leader and is not given lightly, that is why it should be highly prized. You demonstrate both passion for the job and compassion for the people. You say what you mean and you do what you say. This will result in gaining the trust of others and they will follow your lead.

Your availability to resolve both work and personal issues in a timely way, your willingness to join the team on the front lines to resolve conflicts, your proven openness and candor on difficult issues, how you backup your words with actions, will determine how you are perceived by members of your team. The team needs to have confidence in you as a leader and needs to respect you as a person. Then you can lead them through difficult challenges.

The American Bald Eagle was centered on the Great Seal of the United States to represent the integrity of a nation.

" If once you forfeit the confidence of your fellow citizens, you can never regain their respect and esteem."

Abraham Lincoln

Part 8.
Actions & Behaviors Define
The Leader

You have developed the attributes of a strong leader, and your actions and behaviors reflect these attributes. Leaders are people who are action oriented. They willingly take on the most difficult tasks and set the hardest goals. They drive results through good judgment and thoughtful decision making.

Leaders go to the front lines of the toughest problems and ask probing questions. They are seeking a solution and believe in hard work and perseverance rather than luck. When coming face to face with tough news, they control their emotions and are never nasty or abusive. They treat everyone with respect and dignity. They deal with the issues, not the personalities. Leaders avoid politics and concentrate on delivering results.

The legacy of an excellent leader is framed by the world-class products delivered to the market and their positive impact on the global economy, the environment, and people's lives.

<u>Discussion Points</u>

1, Takes Big Swings
2. Takes A Position - Makes A Point
3. Believes In Hard Work Versus Luck
4. Goes To The Front Lines Of Tough Problems
5. Asks Probing Questions
6. Negotiates Face To Face On Tough Issues
7. Maintains Control Of Emotions
8. Is Never Nasty Or Abusive
9. Avoids The Politics
10. Shows The Way Towards A Better Future

Takes Big Swings

Think big, take on the toughest tasks and manage risk. To hit a home run in any business or project we must take a big swing, but realize that every big swing will not produce a home run.

In 1920 Babe Ruth not only hit more home runs that any player, he hit more home runs than any team in the league. He showed it wasn't all about bunting, singles, and base stealing; the big swing paid off. He changed the game by introducing something no one had expected. He set himself apart from the rest of the league. Financially, he made five times the salary of any other player. The customers came to see him. The new Yankee Stadium, became known as "The House That Ruth Built." Your innovation should change the game in its market: don't bunt, go for the fences.

The impossible is possible. Go after the biggest fish, and as in the case of this Great Blue Heron, its capture will bring the greatest satisfaction.

"I swing big with everything I've got. I hit big or I miss big. I like to live as big as I can."

Babe Ruth

Takes a Position - Makes a Point

You have a contribution to make and it could well change the direction of the team. You need to speak up and put your opinions on the table, and then listen carefully to the discussion before responding.

Sometimes we are too fearful of raising an issue and causing conflict. It is always preferable to address and solve an issue earlier in a product cycle, before large amounts of money are spent, and later change will certainly be more costly and less welcome.

Be true to your beliefs; it's sometimes necessary to take an unpopular position. Sometimes more upfront investment in people and technology are required, and you need to share your reasoning to avoid a disaster. You will not regret the things you did say, you will only regret the things you did not say. Speak out clearly for what you believe, be decisive, make your voice heard. Take a position on the key issues, or your fuzzy words or silence will be taken for consent.

"When eagles are silent, the parrots begin to jabber."

Sir Winston Churchill

Believes In Hard Work Versus Luck

Thomas Edison talked about how some of his critics accused him of just being lucky. His response was that his achievements were founded on hard work, not luck, and the difference between himself and those talking about luck was they gave up, and he never did.

When taking on a difficult project I have found that working the hardest during the concept phase is the most critical. The key is to identify a concept that can inherently make the targets, and at the same time, identify the risk areas. Most risks will come in areas of new technology, and this can be mitigated in two ways. The first is to precisely track all the technology programs you are counting on. In one project I led, this amounted to 53 rigs and development efforts. The second is to define fallback positions so that one technology roadblock doesn't scuttle the whole project. If a technology program falls behind, you will know it immediately. You can redouble the effort, or you can employ the backup plan.

A project always has unanticipated difficulties and also things that go better than expected. The more effort put in upfront in doing your homework, tracking technology programs, providing backup plans, and building rigs and prototypes, the better the project will flow. This approach will greatly minimize the number of unanticipated problems. When a surprise does occur, stay calm, gather information quickly, tell yourself the truth, and make a decision to correct the issue.

"Most Fellows try a few things and quit, I never quit till I get what I'm after. That's the only difference between me, that supposed to be lucky, and the fellows that think their unlucky."

Thomas Edison

Goes To The Front Lines Of Tough Problems

You need to lead from the bow, not the stern, of the ship. You can't know and understand a key problem from the comfort of your office. The initial information and recommended solution should come from your direct reports. Experience shows, however, that in difficult situations there is a reluctance to ask for more resources or to reveal the depth of the problem at hand.

You must visit the front lines and talk to the people who are doing the job. Put aside all other work and concentrate fully on the problem at hand. Only then can you appreciate the depth and breadth of the problem and the elements of its potential solution. Many leaders fail this test and deal only with their direct reports; this is a recipe for failure.

I have found situations where a team felt so overwhelmed by the depth and breadth of their problems that they were willing to quit. It was necessary to help them structure a recovery plan with additional resources and higher priority to get their improved hardware manufactured. These are things they could not have done on their own. In addition your personal involvement, commitment, and words of encouragement will inspire the team. Spend your time dealing with and resolving the most difficult issues and delegate the rest. That's what separates good leadership from great leadership.

_____

" His cardinal mistake is that he isolates himself, and allows nobody to see him; and by which he does not know what is going on in the very matter he is dealing with."

Abraham Lincoln

Asks Probing Questions

Thomas Edison was forced out of school early in his youth for asking too many questions. Albert Einstein was forced to leave high school because he also asked too many questions that irritated his teachers, who apparently were only interested in rote learning.

Questions and challenges to the status quo are what's needed to advance the state of the art, leading to breakthrough ideas, and new products. Children are born questioners, and this behavior should be strongly encouraged. Einstein said that his great advantage over other physicists was that he kept asking childlike questions well into his adulthood. One of those great questions was "what would the world look like if I could ride on a beam of light." The answer that came to him was that time itself would stand still. This became an integral part of his theory of special relativity in 1905.

In caring for my grandchildren I was often amazed by the insightful questions they asked. After swimming in lakes and oceans they wondered, "why are the oceans salty but the lakes not salty." When I was explaining the naming of the planets after the Greek and Roman gods they asked, "why is the Earth called the Earth." I had to search hard for the answers.

Questions are the key to understanding and we should not be hesitant when asking them even if they result in some initial friction. Stand up and ask the question!

"The important thing is to not stop questioning. -- One cannot help but be in awe when he contemplates the mysteries of eternity, of life, of the marvelous structure of reality. -- never lose a holy curiosity."

Albert Einstein

Negotiates Face To Face On Tough Issues

On difficult issues a face to face meeting can achieve a resolution much sooner than written or phone communication. Body language and facial expressions don't communicate via email or text message. Listening is key: always attempt to thoroughly understand another person's stated position before you offer a counter proposal.

Preparation for an important face to face meeting is critical. Gather all the relevant details. Establish an entry position, but be flexible when and where appropriate. Admit when you're wrong and have the courage to change direction. The goal should be to first select and agree on the right overall direction at a high level, and then work your way down through the details, gaining as much consensus as possible.

Use this one on one meeting to address the issues openly and honestly and turn a confrontation into a working relationship.

"Let us never negotiate out of fear but let us never fear to negotiate."

John F. Kennedy

Maintains Control Of Emotions

There are times when something will be said or done that makes us angry. This is a test of leadership. You need to address the issue that's driving the anger in a manner that leads to a correction of the issue rather than one that causes further difficulties.

Think clearly and thoughtfully before speaking. The fastest response is usually not the best answer. The higher the level of leadership you attain, the more weight your team will give to every one of your words.

Do not be intimidated by shouting and pounding on the table, but stick to the facts and make your counter-point firmly and with unwavering conviction. You are supported by the facts and your opponent's anger typically reveals his or her lack of a genuine counter-point.

Address the issue and do not be offensive, even if faced with character attacks. Keep pushing the conversation back to the unresolved issue. Take the high road. Do not lower yourself to the realm of personal attacks.

Maintain your respect for others and your dignity, even though others may lose theirs. Speak passionately, make your point, and preserve your civility. You can't expect to successfully lead others if you can't control your own emotions.

"When angry, count to ten before you speak; if very angry, one hundred."

Thomas Jefferson

94

Is Never Nasty Or Abusive

When a leader displays a nasty behavior, it has an extremely negative effect on the environment that is required to develop innovative people and products. It can defeat many other positive attributes that you may possess.

I have observed cases where people have worked extremely hard on a new technology, delivered an excellent working prototype, and made a thoughtful presentation to senior management, only to have their idea tossed out without due consideration of its benefits. If this wasn't bad enough, the people making the presentation were not treated respectfully, considering the huge amount of effort they put forward. Many times, the root cause of this bad behavior lies in company politics that are completely hidden from the presenting team. Often politics results in bad decisions because it's not based on good judgment, but on selfish interests, instead.

If you don't agree that a technology should continue to be supported, you need to clearly make the points that support that position. Thank the team for their effort, and tell them that every great effort does not lead to a marketable product. Make an effort to thank them individually and provide encouragement for their future endeavors.

There is no acceptable excuse for nasty or abusive behavior to be directed at any decent human being.

"The pursuit of truth does not permit violence on one's opponent."

Mahatma Gandhi

Avoids The Politics

Earn your advancement based on leading innovative change in products, and processes, and acquiring and developing talented people. You have rotated through many assignments, and your broad experience has been recognized by your supervisors in many departments.

You have accepted the most challenging assignments, worked through difficult issues, and delivered excellent results. Negative words said by others cannot replace your track record of delivering on the goals and objectives. You have avoided making decisions based on political considerations and, instead, based them on first principles. Let these results speak for themselves.

You have developed and mentored young talented associates who are making real contributions. These people will participate in upward evaluations that will reflect positively on your leadership attributes.

Treat your bosses, your peers, and those that work for you with equal respect and dignity. Avoid speaking negatively of others; instead, you should emphasize your teams accomplishments, your leadership, and your vision for both the business and yourself. It is correct to say that he who lives by the sword, dies by the sword. Politics and back stabbing are not a sound foundation on which to build a future. Move upward based on results and integrity.

"Politics are almost as exciting as war, and -- quite as dangerous. -- In war you can only be killed once, but in politics many times."

Sir Winston Churchill

Shows the Way Towards
A Better Future

When we recognize a need for change, we should step up and make a proposal. It takes courage to be the one to stand up at a meeting and put the first proposal on the table. Let others take their shots at it—absorb their criticisms and modify your plan as appropriate. This will build consensus.

Those ideas that change the direction of an important, ingrained project are the hardest to sell; but, they are the most critical. You will face strong resistance from vested interests, but continuing on the wrong track is unacceptable. You have explained why the current direction of a project is unacceptable. If your idea is rejected, then what do your critics propose? Hope and wishful thinking will not save the day. Big problems require big changes.

Lead, make the first proposal, draw the first sketch, show the way.

"If we don't change our direction, we are likely to end up where we are headed."

Chinese Proverb

Part 9.
Working On Self Improvement

Self-improvement is a journey that is taken over a lifetime. Your ability to achieve increased leadership responsibility will depend on growing your strengths and eliminating your weaknesses. To do this, you must be able to face the mirror and do an honest self-evaluation. George Washington Carver said it this way, *"Most people search high and wide for the keys to success. If they only knew, the key to their dreams lies within."*

You need to achieve excellent results on your current project and then seek jobs of increasing challenge and responsibility. The more difficult the assignment, the more you can learn and grow. Don't fill the entire day with meetings, email, and texting and never have time to quietly and intensely analyze key issues. Be sure to allow yourself time alone to think.

In the end, you will develop experience achieving tough goals. This will give you confidence to trust your intuition and make excellent judgments and decisions.

Discussion Points

1. Practice Self-Reflection
2. Believe In Yourself
3. Develop A Proactive Style
4. Allow Yourself Time To Think
5. Have Your Own "Thinking Place"
6. Learn From Experience
7. Practice Life Long Learning
8. Balance Work And Home Responsibilities
9. Know Relativity
10. Learn To Soar

Practice Self-Reflection

Self-reflection is a necessary process to assure that you are working on continuously improving your skills and correcting your weaknesses. In this regard, your toughest critics can provide the most useful insights. They may point out faults that you consider attributes, however, they may also provide truthful and constructive suggestions for change.

It is important to access your capabilities relative to both relationships and projects. Are you being asked to do the most difficult projects? Do people seek out and respect your opinion? If not, why not?

It's not just about leading change to improve a company's products and processes: it's also about improving yourself. Look in the mirror and be truthful about the positives and negatives you see.

"There are three things extremely hard: steel, a diamond, and to know one's self."

Benjamin Franklin

Believe In Yourself

As you gain knowledge and experience you will build your self-confidence and begin to trust you intuition and good judgment. The more you trust yourself, the more you will be willing to strike off in a new direction, the more daring you will be, and the greater the results you will deliver.

You will enter new assignments with a high level of confidence. You are not afraid to wade into new waters: you meet new people, and discuss new technology. You can research any subject pertinent to your project and converse intelligently with the experts in that field.

You confidently address the most difficult issues. You are on the front lines helping to resolve them. You can simplify a complex set of problems and present a solution that everyone can buy into.

Believing in yourself doesn't mean going it alone. You believe in your ability to choose the right people for each assignment. You know you will stay close to them and inspire them going forward.

You are decisive! When it's time to launch a new concept, waiting for the last 10% of the information is aptly called "analysis paralysis." Never wait—either you're actively gathering information or your launching new ideas.

"We must have -- above all confidence in ourselves. We must believe that we are gifted for something, and that this thing, at whatever the cost, must be obtained."

Marie Curie

Develop A Proactive Style

Leaders go out and make things happen. They bubble over with a contagious energy and enthusiasm. They never sit on the side lines and just let things happen and whine later when expectations are not met.

Decide every morning on the way to work what needs to be accomplished that day. Check your calendar, rearrange things if necessary. Set up the meetings that need to happen immediately, write the emails to stir the pot early in the day, and make the necessary phone calls without delay. A calendar cannot be fixed in stone, because the priorities of yesterday are not the priorities of today. Stay flexible and adjust to changing events.

Develop a list of the top-ten problems in your area of responsibility. Place a trusted leader in charge of each one. Visit these leaders often to assess progress and drive results. Never back off until the root cause is found and the solution is imminent.

Be responsive to customer complaints. You may need to form an industry team if the problem is found to be broad based. Check with customers that don't have the problem— they may have a solution you can use. See that the problem fix is affordable, or it will not be fielded.

Determine to make things happen every day.

"There are people who make things happen, there are people who watch things happen, and there are people who wonder what happened."

Proverb

Allow Yourself Time To Think

You can easily become a slave to your email and calendar and fill your day with routine chores. We have all spent days wading through a swamp of bureaucratic emails and attending "information only" meetings, and thereby accomplishing none of our stretch goals or objectives. Don't let this happen. Allow yourself time to think creatively every day.

You can't solve a daunting problem, or overcome an innovation roadblock, without setting time aside to weigh all the particulars and to outline a recovery plan. You need to determine which team leaders and technical specialists to meet with. Which partners or customers need to be informed of the problem? What additional resources need to be applied? By taking the time to think creatively, we can proactively address issues as they arise.

Creative thinking time is not restricted to an office environment, it may occur on a daily jog, in the shower, or at 30,000 ft. over the ocean in an airplane, where you have time to let your thoughts flow freely. Keep a notebook or tablet and record your ideas and come back to them again and again. Each time you will be able to expand and improve on them, Your subconscious mind will be working on these ideas even while you are doing other tasks.

The best ideas may come to you when all the duties of a typical day are put aside and your mind expands beyond today into a promising tomorrow.

" I think and think for months and years. Ninety nine times the conclusion is false. The hundred time I am right."

Albert Einstein

Have Your Own "Thinking Place"

You need a special space of quiet solitude where you can let your mind be free to explore new ideas. Take the toughest unsolved problems into your thinking place and you will find new approaches to resolve them. Once you do this successfully, your confidence will soar, and this place will become a recognized and well used asset. Know your body rhythms and set aside time in which your creative side can flourish. Surround yourself with an environment that encourages creativity and bold thinking. The elements in this place are combined to permit an intense, creative focus and concentration. It can be a special room in your home or an inspiring place outside.

Alexander Graham Bell had the breakthrough inspiration for the telephone at his "dreaming place" behind his parent's house.

"It would be possible to transmit sounds of any sort if we could only occasion a variation in the intensity of the current exactly like that occurring in the density of air while a given sound is made."

Alexander Graham Bell

Learn From Experience

We are guided in decision making by our dreams, our technical knowledge of first principles, by our moral code of ethics, and also by our intuition. Intuition is based on experience, and the more broad and diverse our experience, the more valuable our intuition.

Job rotation is an important tool in gaining broader experience. There are areas in the new department that you haven't seen before, and will struggle with in the beginning. These struggles build character and confidence.

Volunteer for a tough assignment. Take the more adventurous road, the one less traveled, and explore some unfamiliar territory. This is how you grow your intuitive capabilities through experience.

" I have but one lamp by which my feet are guided; and that is the lamp of experience."

Patrick Henry

Practice Life Long Learning

We start learning as a child from our parents and in our local schools. We may graduate from college and we take appropriate post graduate courses and degrees. When our formal education is over, we have only just begun the learning process. Every job assignment, every training course, every person we meet, every international partnering experience, is an opportunity to learn.

Take full advantage of the training courses and rotation programs, your company offers. You need to have a plan of development for yourself, and then decide what company courses are aligned with that plan. Many companies have rotation programs to enable you to see a broad spectrum of the work they perform in order to find your best fit. Even if an official rotation program does not exist, many companies offer posting opportunities. I found that by rotating through the design groups of almost all the components in an engine, I was well qualified to lead a systems integration team for the whole engine.

Subscribe to the magazines that are the accepted standard for your industry. Keep up with the products and technologies in your industry. Know what the competition is offering. Today we have outstanding college level courses, taught by the world's most capable professors, available to us on formats such as DVD and on the internet. Choose an area of improvement and enjoy one of these learning experiences. Learning and improving is a lifelong process: it's a journey, not a destination.

"Wisdom is not a product of schooling but of the lifelong attempt to acquire it."

Albert Einstein

Balance Work And Home Responsibilities

Carefully consider the impact of any new policy effecting your employees. Do not issue edicts that are good for you, but damage the lives, ambitions, and fundamental rights of your team members. Share the proposal with your team members and seek their input and support.

Personal issues outside of work can have an adverse effect on one's work performance. Supporting a team member in a family crisis is the right thing to do and will pay big dividends in the long run.

Assure that each team member takes their needed vacation and holiday time, and you will be rewarded with many examples of perfect year end attendance. Be mindful and respectful of a work-life balance for you and your team.

" We hold these truths to be self-evident: that all men are created equal; that they are endowed by their creator with certain unalienable rights; that among these are life, liberty, and the pursuit of happiness --

Thomas Jefferson

Know Relativity

The relationship between ethics, people, process, and innovation may be reduced to integrity. We must start our organization with a leader of the highest integrity if we are to achieve the breakthrough innovations that we desire.

Thomas Edison and Walt Disney had the unquestioned respect and admiration of their team members. They earned it by always being there on the front lines in the toughest situations and by always keeping their promises. When Snow White was a huge success, Walt paid his team members the bonuses he had promised them, despite strong suggestions that the finances of the business would suffer.

Integrity is a characteristic that is formulated and earned over time and cannot be added later. Rather, it is built up in ourselves through many years of diligent and creative effort and caring for the rights of others.

Our integrity is best seen in the opinions and feelings of those that work with us and for us. It's not something we measure directly, but could be assessed in an indirect way. If you were put in charge of a new division, would your team leaders and associates ask to go with you?

When you become a person of value, everyone wants you on their team or wants to be part of your team. You are a strong contributor to the well-being of society and mankind.

_____

" Try to become not a man(person) of success, but try rather to become a man(person) of value."

Albert Einstein

Learn To Soar

You have expanded your technical and leadership capabilities with every new job assignment. You have volunteered for the more difficult assignments and accepted opportunities to move within the company. This difficult path you have traveled has increased the scope of your knowledge while creating important additional supporters of your growth potential. Do not level off and get complacent, instead, continue to be proactive in all you do.

As you have gained cross discipline experience in successfully completing challenging leadership assignments, you will have increased the scope of future responsibilities that you can confidently take on. Get comfortable with your experience and knowledge and learn to depend on your intuition and good judgment. You could decide to strike off and found your own company. Why not?

Learn to soar like an eagle and you will accomplish more than you thought was possible. Be all you can be.

"The more one does and sees and feels, the more one is able to do."

Amelia Earhart

Part 10.
Projecting The Future

There are two fundamental approaches to projecting the future:

Evolutionary: By extending existing trends through continuous parametric improvements.

Disruptive: Through game-changing new technology that makes existing systems obsolete.

Most change occurs in an evolutionary way. Products are introduced that improve speed, accuracy, cost, and comfort. To be a world leader in evolutionary changes requires continuously developing the design and manufacturing technologies and processes that will set your product apart. It requires bench marking the competition and correctly projecting where they are going in both the short and long-term. It requires a culture that welcomes change and encourages the hiring and nurturing of innovative people.

Disruptive changes are harder to predict; they can wipe out an industry overnight. Digital cameras, for example, have almost totally replaced film cameras. The film making and developing industry is disappearing. I believe that disruptive changes are predictable if we take what I will call a "Jules Vernian" view. Jules Verne was a French science fiction writer of the mid-eighteenth century. His books: *20,000 Leagues Under the Sea*, and *From the Earth to The Moon*, predict a future world with unexpected accuracy. In From the Earth To The Moon, he envisions three men, launched from Florida, journeying to the Moon. He gets the launch location right, the escape velocity right, he anticipates zero gravity, and he gets the material of the capsule right, aluminum. He combines his imagination with scientific fact. He hires artillery mathematicians to correctly calculate the escape velocity and determine the weight of the capsule.

Alexander Graham Bell correctly forecast in 1917 that the unchecked burning of fossil fuels would result in a greenhouse effect. Thomas Edison in 1931 correctly forecast the promise of solar energy in a world of dwindling coal and oil supplies. He wished he had more years left to develop it. The future is predicable if we combine our imagination with our latest knowledge and project them in an unbiased way.

The future represents challenges that we must be ready to take on with optimism and confidence. Robert Goddard, the father of rocket propulsion, said in his high school oration, *"It is difficult to say what is impossible, for the dream of yesterday is the hope of today and the reality of tomorrow."*

Discussion Points

1. Take A "Jules Vernian" View
2. Focus On The Future
3. Become A Radial Thinker And Achiever
4. Think Disruptive Change
5. Have An Innovation Lab For Prototyping
6. Accept That The Impossible Is Possible
7. Realize That The Experts Can Be Wrong
8. Have The Courage To Fly Alone
9. Make That Leap Into Unknown Territory
10. Enjoy The Thrill Of Victory

Take A "Jules Vernian" View

Jules Verne, a French science fiction writer of the mid eighteenth century, used his imagination, and combined it with the most advanced scientific principles of his time, to predict both the nuclear powered submarine, and the journey to the Moon, one hundred years before they happened. The US Navy named the world's first nuclear powered submarine the Nautilus, after the submarine of that name in Verne's *20,000 Leagues Under The Sea*. In recognition of the vision of Jules Verne, a copy of his novel, From the *Earth To The Moon*, along with some original manuscripts, have been placed aboard the International Space Station.

The future is predictable: Jules Verne has proven that. Catch the uplifting currents of tomorrow. A combination of imagination, the latest scientific knowledge, and practical logic can reveal the future in terms of both evolutionary and disruptive changes.

"Anything one man can imagine other men can make real."

Jules Verne

Focus On The Future

Our innovations will provide an improved future state. We can create evolutionary changes by projecting the trends of key parameters, and anticipating the environment that that our innovations will be born into. We can originate disruptive changes by creating an innovation lab and encouraging breakthrough thinking.

To be a world leader in evolutionary change requires continuously developing the design and manufacturing technologies and processes that will set our product apart. Understanding customer expectations and competitor offerings and always providing more than expected in total product value will be defining attributes.

Disruptive changes will require more radical thinking and approaches, and combined with a spirit of daring, will yield a much greater reward. These changes do not typically come from the normal working environment, but originate in innovation labs, where there are fundamentally "no rules" and people can explore revolutionary ideas and concepts.

Look forward, invest in technology, take a confident and fearless aim at the future. Assure that your planned new products will play a leading role in changing the world.

"It's important to imagine the demands of each generation and accordingly, to work looking ten years into the future. You have to face the future and think what will be important or necessary at that time."

Akio Morita

Become A Radial Thinker
And Achiever

Breakthrough thinkers like Leonardo da Vinci, Thomas Edison, Albert Einstein, George Washington Carver, and Walt Disney, had these characteristics in common:

- They challenged existing experts in their field
- They searched for answers to the toughest questions
- The spent long hours of hard work looking for a breakthrough
- They accepted that many failures would precede a solution
- They combined logic and the imagination to achieve a breakthrough
- They used system level thinking

Think and act boldly. Stick your neck out: progress is made by pursuing stretch goals.

"We must dare to be great; and we must realize that greatness is the fruit of toil and sacrifice and high courage."

Theodore Roosevelt

Think Disruptive Change

Disruptive changes are those that make existing products obsolete, often overnight. Jet flight between continents made all existing competing venues obsolete. Electronic watches made mechanical watches obsolete. Digital cameras made film cameras obsolete. iPods made CD's obsolete. If you don't want to be left behind, you must be pursuing disruptive changes.

Hire especially creative and disruptive thinkers. Let them work in a special environment of minimum rules and open communication. See that they don't get dragged down by bureaucratic paperwork and endless reporting. Give them a prototyping ability. Create a flat organization structure in which decisions can be made on the spot. Assure that their ideas are seen by senior managers.

We want unconventional thinkers for our disruptive team. They will be unconventional in the hours they work, their dress code, and their diversity will be apparent in every area. The great disruptive thinkers were not a fit for society's norm. Einstein wore no socks, Edison slept on his roll top desk, Disney had a small working railroad installed on his property. None of them worked normal hours.

Build a prototype of fully integrated components aimed at the new user experience. Try it out on selected customers, make necessary changes, and launch it into the market. Be bold, be courageous.

"Courage is the main quality of leadership -- Usually it implies some risk -- especially in new undertakings. Courage to initiate something and to keep it going, pioneering and adventurous spirit to blaze new ways."

Walt Disney

Have An Innovation Lab
For Prototyping

An innovation lab is a small group of bold and creative people, of different disciplines, that can take an idea or concept and build a working prototype. They operate in an open environment of minimum bureaucracy, with all of the necessary disciplines co-located. The result is a capability to deliver a breakthrough concept with 10% of the people, at 10% of the cost, and a fraction of the time that would normally be required.

Thomas Edison established the world's first innovation lab at Menlo Park. Here he created and modified prototypes of his great inventions in less time, at lower cost, and with fewer people then would normally be required. From this lab came breakthrough products such as the electric light bulb and the phonograph. Using today's 3D printers, rapid prototyping can be taken to the next level. An innovation lab is the best way to support both evolutionary and disruptive technology. It is a model of agility and cost effectiveness.

Kelly Johnson created the modern version of Menlo Park with his famous "skunk works" at Lockheed. Here is where his team gathered around the concept, sharing ideas, focused on results, building prototypes until their dream became a reality. Out of the skunk works came daring new concepts such as the SR71 Blackbird spy-plane of the cold war, and the stealth fighter.

"For some time I have been pestering -- to let me set up an experimental department where designers and shop artisans could work together closely in the development of airplanes without the delays and complications of intermediate departments --."

Clarence L. *"Kelly"* Johnson

Accept That The Impossible Is Possible

Leading scientists of the late 19th century stated emphatically that heavier than air flying machines were not possible, but a few years later the Wright brothers flew anyway. They ignored the negativity and turned their dream into reality.

For many years engineers could not explain how bumble bees could hover, considering their weight and wing capacity. But bumble bees do hover, and with modern scientific tools we can understand how this is possible. Nature only reveals her secrets after years of diligent hard work and bold thinking.

Landing a man on the moon in less than ten years was considered impossible by most people. They thought President Kennedy wasn't serious when he announced a lunar mission in the early 1960's. But John Kennedy was serious, and so was the leadership of NASA.

"Houston, Tranquility Base here, The Eagle has landed." -- That's one small step for man, one giant leap for mankind."

Neil Armstrong

Realize That The Experts
Can Be Wrong

Experts can have too narrow a vision and don't see or welcome the new approach you are bringing to the table. The new disciplines that will be required to perfect your invention may be outside their areas of expertise. This can make their discipline much less important and divert technology money from their projects to yours. Try to separate constructive criticism from stone walling. Listen well to their challenges, address their issues where appropriate, and proceed with your project.

A wise old owl, may not share your vision, but your tenacity and belief in your project can carry the day. Some of the most respected thinkers of a given time in history have been dead wrong. It was only seven years after Lord Kelvin made his thoughts on controlled flight known that the Wright Brothers proved him wrong.

"I have not the smallest molecule of faith in aerial navigation other than ballooning."

Lord Kelvin (1896)

Have The Courage To Fly Alone

You have an idea that others do not immediately agree with and some openly oppose. You should not discard it. Write it down and keep working it in your thinking place.

The best innovative ideas did not receive early recognition and the inventors kept them alive with the courage of their convictions, resourcefulness, and a spirit of adventure. Tesla built the first electric automobile with a range of 200 miles, a feat other competitors thought was impossible. They are selling their cars without the conventional dealership building. They had the courage to fly alone.

When RAF pilot Frank Whittle patented his concept for the jet(gas turbine) engine in 1930, he did not receive the recognition or support from the British aviation authorities that one might have expected. They calculated a jet engine could not replace a piston engine due to weight and other factors. They were wrong. Frank kept his idea alive and ran the world's first successful jet engine in 1937. He revolutionized airplane power plant design and made supersonic flight possible.

Be persistent and there will be an opportunity to develop and build your innovation. When your first success arrives, it will only increase your desire to fly even higher in search of new concepts.

" I began to feel that I lived on a higher plane than the skeptics of the ground; one that was richer because of its very association with the element of danger -- In flying I tasted the wine of the Gods of which they could know nothing."

Charles A. Lindbergh

Make That Leap Into Unknown Territory

Take bold action, create and deploy a disruptive change. Be willing to explore unknown territory and take the big risk for the big reward. The first airplane flight, the first affordable car, the first full length carton feature, the first electronic computer, the first step out on to the lunar surface, the first modern electric car, the first smart phone—each opened up a new world of opportunity.

Walt Disney bet his company many times on a bold new idea that required a leap into unknown territory. The first full length animated motion picture, Snow White, the first theme park of immense scope and proportions, Disneyland, and the first full length movie combining actors and animation, Mary Poppins. Walt Disney's innovations changed the world and made it a better place .Spread your wings and make that flight into the unknown, where lies a new and brighter future. Don't be constrained by the negative comments and doubts of others.

"The only limit to our realization of tomorrow will be our doubts of today."

Franklin Roosevelt

Enjoy The Thrill Of Victory

It's fun to achieve what others think is impossible.

Jump for joy, celebrate!—you and your team made it happen.
There is no better feeling.

*"Happiness lies not in the mere possession of money, it lies in
the joy of achievement, in the thrill of creative effort."*

Franklin Roosevelt

Epilogue

"No individual has any right to come into the world and go out of it without leaving behind -- distinct and legitimate reasons for having passed through it"

George Washington Carver

Self-Improvement Test

This is a self-scoring test. There are 10 chapters in this book, each with 10 sections, for a total of 100 sections. If you feel you currently achieve the section behavior or recommendation you score it a "yes." A perfect score would be a "yes" to each section, or 100 "yeses" equal 100%. This test is intended to help you focus on areas that you can improve and strengthen.

Part 1. Developing A Vision

    1. Aim Your Product Goal At World Leadership
    2. Be A Visionary Dreamer
    3. Dedicate Time For Imagination & Fantasy
    4. Choose A New Direction
    5. Leap Frog The Competition
    6. Present Your Vision
    7. Overcome The Initial Resistance To Change
    8. Recognize The Tipping Point
    9. Stay Customer Focused
  10. Vision + Daring + Conviction = Success

Part 2. Establishing An Innovation Team

    1. Turn Vision Into Action
    2. Select A Team Of High Integrity
    3. Treat Every Team Member As Important
    4. Build A Team of Diverse & Creative Thinkers
    5. Create Responsibility Centers
    6. Match Peoples Skills To Their Assignments
    7. Respect Cultural Differences
    8. Assure Team Alignment
    9. Optimize Teamwork
  10. Achieve A Synergy of Team Effort

Part 3. Inspiring An Innovation Team
     1. Lead By Example
     2. Motivate Your Team
     3. Practice Open Communication & Transparency
     4. Walk In Your Associates Moccasins
     5. Realize That Fear & Innovation Are Incompatible
     6. Value Hard Work
     7. Give Recognition & Reward At Key Milestones
     8. Coach & Mentor Future Leaders
     9. End Every Meeting With Action Items Assigned
    10. Love The Work

Part 4. Developing Key Strategies
     1. Tell The Truth Up Front
     2. Take A Results View
     3. Strive To Deliver The Finest Results
     4. Gather New Data To Support Decisions
     5. Seek Independent Expert Critique
     6. Make Timely Decisions Based On First Principles
     7. Take Prudent Risks
     8. Don't Take Foolish Risks
     9. Value Your Time
    10. Know Your Competitor

Part 5. Elements Of An Innovative Product
     1. Creates An Industry
     2. Solves A Known Customer Need
     3. Provides A New User Experience
     4. Provides A Better Mouse Trap
     5. Recognizes The Interconnectivity Of All Things
     6. Recognizes The Synergy Of Product Components
     7. Features A Simple And Elegant Product Design
     8. Features A Breakthrough Concept

    9. Is Demonstrated By A Prototype
  10. Has 90% Of Its Value Set By The Concept Choice

[ ]

Part 6. Delivering The Innovative Product
    1. Step Out Of Your Comfort Zone
    2. Be A Force For Positive Change
    3. Confront The Unreasonable Critic
    4. Be Prepared To Cross Difficult Roads
    5. Monitor Progress - Don't Accept Smiles
    6. Recognize A Key Issue When Others Do Not
    7. Address A Problem Before It's Too Late To Fix
    8. Take A leadership Role In A Crisis
    9. Advocate For Continuous Innovation
  10. Attitude -Program Failure Can Not Be An Option

[ ]

Part 7. Attributes That Enable A Leader
    1. Systems Level Thinker
    2. Self-Confident & Decisive
    3. Committed To Excellence
    4. Courageous & Bold
    5. Optimistic & Resourceful
    6. Diligent & Persistent
    7, Opportunistic
    8. Vigilant
    9. Excellent Communicator
  10. Respected By All - Integrity

[ ]

Part 8. Actions & Behaviors Define The Leader
    1, Takes Big Swings
    2. Takes A Position - Makes A Point
    3. Believes In Hard Work Versus Luck
    4. Goes To The Front Lines Of Tough Problems
    5. Asks Probing Questions
    6. Negotiates Face To Face On Tough Issues

7. Maintains Control Of Emotions
8. Is Never Nasty Or Abusive
9. Avoids The Politics
10. Shows The Way Towards A Better Future

☐

Part 9. Working On Self Improvement
1. Practice Self-Reflection
2. Believe In Yourself
3. Develop A Proactive Style
4. Allow Yourself Time To Think
5. Have Your Own "Thinking Place"
6. Learn From Experience
7. Practice Life Long Learning
8. Balance Work And Home Responsibilities
9. Know Relativity
10. Learn To Soar

☐

Part 10. Projecting The Future
1. Take A "Jules Vernian" View
2. Focus On The Future
3. Become A Radial Thinker And Achiever
4. Think Disruptive Change
5. Have An Innovation Lab For Prototyping
6. Accept That The Impossible Is Possible
7. Realize That The Experts Can Be Wrong
8. Have The Courage To Fly Alone
9. Make That Leap Into Unknown Territory
10. Enjoy The Thrill Of Victory

☐

Total ☐

Acknowledgments

I want to thank my wife and partner, Janice, for her support and dedication to this effort. Her excellent pictures and advice helped make this book possible.

I also wish to thank my daughters, Karen and Susan, for their careful review and thoughtful advice on how to improve the contents of this book.

About The Author

The author is a retired chief engineer of systems design, and chief engineer of the Pratt & Whitney division of United Technologies Corporation (UTC), where he worked for 36 years. He holds a bachelors and masters degree in mechanical engineering and has received 13 US patents.

He has completed the Management of Technology Change, and the Promoting Innovation graduate courses at the Massachusetts Institute of Technology. He has also completed the University of Virginia Darden School - Senior Executive Program.

During his career he has been recruited to solve some of the most difficult problems faced by his and other divisions of UTC, and has a wealth of experience in leading international teams to develop innovative solutions to the toughest problems. He received an ASME Engineer of the Year Award in 1998 for his efforts in aerospace engineering.

In his most difficult assignment he received an overall leadership rating of six out of a possible six from eight of eleven team members. The product of the team's effort received a prestigious national award, the Collier Trophy.

He has given lectures on Systems Engineering and Integrated Product Development at the Massachusetts Institute of Technology and Boston University respectively. He has also lectured at the University of Connecticut on The Challenges of Aerospace Engines.

He is currently a member of Chaplin Consulting Services LLC, and writes and teaches courses on leadership, innovation, systems engineering, and the art of design. He also continues to provide innovative solutions to difficult engineering problems.

The content of this book was developed by Mr. Chaplin as a member of Chaplin Consulting Services based on his experience and represents his best judgment and not necessarily that of any other person or company.

Notes

Preface

"Look deep into nature, and then you will understand everything better." Albert Einstein, to Margot Einstein (1951) quote by Hanna Loewy in A&E Television Einstein Biography, VIP International, 1991.

Part 1. Developing A Vision

"I think many people assume, wrongly, that a company exists simply to make money. -- a group of people get together and exist as -- a company so they are able to accomplish something collectively which they could not accomplish separately. -- they make a contribution to society." David Packard, from a speech to HP Managers(March 8, 1960), from the book The *HP Way*, by David Packard.

"The forward objective is clear cut and no less than obtaining world leadership in aviation power plants." Frederick B. Rentschler (founder of Pratt & Whitney Division of UTC), recorded in the pamphlet *In the company of eagles,* 1990.

"The virtuous man is driven by responsibility, the non-virtuous man is driven by profit." Confucius, *The Analects,* Chapter IV.

"Let us not forget it has been the visionary dreamers who have accomplished more for the edification and benefit of mankind than any other contributor to civilization past or present." Dr. Wernher Von Braun speech, Dedication of Roswell Museum, April 15, 1959, from Powell-Willhite's Book *"The Voice of Dr. Wernher Von Braun"* p57.

"When I examine myself and my methods of thought, I come to the conclusion that the gift of fantasy has meant more to me than my talent for absorbing absolute knowledge." Albert Einstein, quote in Ryan, *Einstein and the Humanities, p125,* from *The Quotable Einstein,* by Alice Calaprice p16.

"Go confidently in the direction of your dreams. Live the life you have imagined." Henry David Thoreau, paraphrased and adapted from his book *Walden,* Wikiquote.

" Far better it is to dare mighty things, to win glorious triumphs, even though checkered by failure, than to take rank with those poor spirits who neither enjoy much or suffer much, because they live in the gray twilight that knows not victory nor defeat." Theodore Roosevelt speech, "The Strenuous Life" before the Hamilton Club in Chicago, April 10, 1899.

"I feel that I have at last struck the solution of a great problem -- and the day is coming when telegraph(telephone) wires will be laid on to houses just like water or gas -- and friends converse with each other without leaving home." Alexander Graham Bell, letter to his father(Mar. 10, 1875), from Dictionary of Canadian Biography Vol. XV.

"I could never convince the financiers that Disneyland was feasible, because dreams offer too little collateral." Walt Disney, from *The Stuff Americans Are Made Of: The Seven Cultural Forces That Define Americans -- ,* by Joshua Hammond and James Morrison(1966).

"The evolvers are people who cause things to change. The maintainers of the status quo do everything to keep things from changing. The numbers of evolvers are much fewer than the maintainers of the status quo -- " Dr. Jonas Salk, Academy of Achievement interview, May 16, 1991, San Diego, CA.

"I will build a car for the great multitude. It will be large enough for the family, but small enough for the individual to run and take care of. It will be constructed of the best materials, by the best men --, after the simplest designs. But it will be so low in price that no man making a good salary will be unable to own one -- Henry Ford, *My Life and Work.*

" For some years I have been afflicted with the belief that flight is possible to man. My disease has increased in severity and I feel it will soon cost me an increased amount of money if not my life." Wilbur Wright, Letter to Octave Chanute, May 13, 1900, Library of Congress.

Part 2. Establishing An Innovation Team

"Vision without action is a daydream. Action without vision is a nightmare." Japanese Proverb, quoted in *Civilization's Quotations: Life's Ideal*(2002) by Richard Alan Krieger, p280.

" Associate yourself with men of good quality if you esteem your own reputation for 'tis better to be alone than in bad company." George Washington, *Rules of Civility,* maxim # 56.

"If it falls to your lot to be a street sweeper, -- sweep the streets like Michelangelo painted pictures, -- and Beethoven composed music, -- sweep the streets so well that all the hosts of heaven and earth will have to pause and say: Here lived a great street sweeper who sweep his job well." Dr. Martin Luther King, speech at the New Covenant Baptist Church, Chicago Ill., April 9, 1967, mlk.stanford.edu.

"No one is thinking if everyone is thinking alike." General George S. Patton, from *General Patton's Principles For Life And Leadership*, by Porter B. Williamson, p. 158.

"We feel our objectives can best be achieved by people who understand what they are trying to do and can utilize their own capabilities to do them." David Packard, from a speech to HP Managers(March 8, 1960), from the book The *HP Way*, by David Packard.

"Of all the things I've done, the most vital is coordinating those who work with me and aiming their efforts at a certain goal." Walt Disney, from *"Walt Disney"* by Neal Gabler, p211.

"Mutual respect is the basis of all civilized human relationships -- it is a requirement in the work one does with one's associates -- it is increasingly necessary in seeking cooperation among the peoples of the world." Eleanor Roosevelt, from her book, "*You Learn by Living*," 1960, p133.

" United we stand: divided we fall." Aesop, from the fable *The Bundle of Sticks,* from the book *The Fables of Aesop, p57,* by Ruth Spriggs.

"Gentleman, we are going to relentlessly chase perfection, knowing full well we will not catch it, because nothing is perfect. But we are going to relentlessly chase it, because in the process we will catch excellence. I am not remotely interested in just being good." Vince Lombardi, from his first team meeting as head coach, reported in *Game of My Life, 25 Stories of Packers Football* (Carlson,2004).

" The whole is more than the sum of its parts." Aristotle, from *Metaphysica,* www- history.mcs.st.and .ac.uk/ Quotations /Aristotle.

Part 3. Inspiring An Innovation Team

" An army of principles will penetrate where an army of soldiers cannot;" Thomas Paine, from his letter to the

Legislature of the French Republic entitled, *Agrarian Justice*(1795-1796).

"Upon this battle depends the survival of Christian civilization -- The whole fury and might of the enemy must very soon be turned on us -- if we fail -- the whole world will sink into the abyss of a new dark age -- Let us therefore brace ourselves to our duties, and so bear ourselves, that if the British empire lasts for a thousand years men will still say, this was their finest hour." Sir Winston Churchill, speech in the House of Commons, June 18, 1940.

" A further important factor in Apollo's success -- was the complete openness with which it was conducted. From top administrators -- to scientists and engineers --, to production workers and even floor sweepers -- , there was an intense feeling of personal responsibility for the success of our mission to the Moon." Dr. Wernher Von Braun speech, Fall Out Effects Of Mega Science, Osaka Japan, March 1971, from Powell-Willhite Book *"The Voice of Dr. Wernher Von Braun"* p175.

" You know, farming looks mighty easy when your plow is a pencil and you're a thousand miles from the corn field." Dwight D. Eisenhower, address, at Bradley University, Peoria, Ill., Sept. 25, 1956.

" Alexander and Caesar, those renown generals received more faithful service, and performed greater actions by means of the love their soldiers bore them, then they could possibly have done, if instead of being -- respected they had been hated and feared by those they commanded." Benjamin Franklin, from his journal of the voyage London to Philadelphia, Wed. July 27, 1726.

"Success can be achieved only through repeated failure and introspection. In fact, success represents 1% of your work, which results only from the 99% that is called failure."

133

Soichiro Honda, from the book *Driving Honda,* by Jeffrey Rothfeder, chapter 1, The Honda Difference.

" This is not the end. It is not even the beginning of the end. But it is, perhaps, the end of the beginning." Sir Winston Churchill speech at Mansion House, November 10, 1942.

"My grandfather once told me that there are two kinds of people: those who do the work and those who take the credit. He told me to try to be in the first group, there was much less competition there." Indira Gandhi, Oct. 1968, New York Times Interview.

"What can be done with care perform today. Dangers unthought of will attend delay." Benjamin Franklin, *Poor Richards Almanack* (1749).

"Disneyland is a work of love. We didn't go into Disneyland just with the idea of making money." Walt Disney, from *The Quotable Walt Disney,* compiled by Dave Smith.

Part 4. Developing Key Strategies

"If I have seen further it is by standing on the shoulders of giants." Sir Isaac Newton letter to Robert Hooke, February 15, 1676.

"Those who fall in love with practice without science are like a sailor who enters a ship without a helm or a compass, and who never can be certain whither he is going." Leonardo da Vinci, from *The Notebooks of Leonardo da Vinci* (Richter, 1888).

"A genius is often merely a talented person who has done all of his or her homework." Thomas Edison, from the book *A Photographic Talk With Edison,* by Theodore Dreiser.

" I have been up against tough competition all my life. I wouldn't know how to get along without it." Walt Disney, from *How To Be Like Walt: Capturing The Magic Every Day of Your Life* by Pat Williams with Jim Denny(2004).

"We choose to go to the moon in this decade -- because that goal will serve to organize and measure the best of our energies and skills, because that challenge is one we are willing to accept, one we are unwilling to postpone,-- therefore, we set sail on the most hazardous and dangerous and greatest adventure on which man has ever embarked." John F. Kennedy speech, Rice University, September 12, 1962.

You always start with a fantasy. Part of the fantasy technique is to visualized something as perfect. Then with experiments you work your way back from fantasy to reality, hacking away at the components." Edwin H. Land, from *Proceedings of the American Philosophical Society*, Vol. 146, p115.

"It takes less time to do a thing right then it does to explain why you did it wrong." Henry Wadsworth Longfellow, widely accepted aphorism.

"You gain strength, courage, and confidence by every experience in which you really stop to look fear in the face.-- you must do the thing you think you can not do." Eleanor Roosevelt, from her book, "You Learn by Living," 1960, p29.

"I think that there is only one quality worse than hardness of heart and that is softness of head." Theodore Roosevelt, Speech at Redding, Cal., May 10, 1903.

"Dost thou love life? Then do not squander time, for that's the stuff life is made of." Benjamin Franklin, *Poor Richard's Almanack(*1746).

Part 5. Elements Of An Innovative Product

" If a man is in need of a rescue, an airplane can come in and throw flowers on him, and that's about all. But a direct lift aircraft can come in and save his life." -- "The helicopter approaches closer than any other vehicle to the fulfillment of man's ancient dream of the flying horse and the magic carpet." Igor Sikorsky, from the Igor Sikorsky Historical Archives, Igor Sikorsky speaks.

"If you sense a deep human need, then you go back to all the basic science. If there is some(thing) missing, then you try and do more basic science and applied science till you get it. So you make the system to fulfill that need --" Edwin H. Land, from *Proceedings of the American Philosophical Society*, Vol. 146, p115.

"It's really hard to design products by focus groups. A lot of times people don't know what they want until you show it to them." Steve Jobs, *Steve Jobs,* Business Week May 12, 1998.

"If a man can write a better book, or preach a better sermon, or build a better mouse trap than his neighbor, though he builds his home in the woods, the world will make a beaten path to his door." Ralph Waldo Emerson, lecture(1871) recorded in *Borrowings,* by Yule and Keane, p. 88.

" The earth is moved from its position by the weight of a tiny bird resting upon it." Leonardo da Vinci, *How To think Like Leonardo da Vinci,* by Michael J. Gelb, p. 222.

" All parts of the system must be constructed with reference to all other parts, since in one sense, all the parts form one

136

machine." Thomas Edison, from *Edison Inventing The Century* by Neil Baldwin, p.103.

"When you first start off trying to solve a problem, the first solutions you come up with are very complex -- But if you keeping going and live with the problem and peel more layers of the onion off, you can often times arrive at some very elegant and simple solutions." Steve Jobs, On the design of the iPod, as quoted in Newsweek (Oct. 14, 2006).

"There is always a way to do it better - find it." Thomas Edison, *Innovate like Edison,* Michael J. Gelb, p72.

"I see a worthwhile need to be met and I make trial after trial until it comes." Thomas Edison, Press Conference(1929), as quoted in *Uncommon Friends: Life with Thomas Edison, Henry Ford, Harvey Firestone, Alexis Carrel & Charles Lindbergh* (1987)by James D. Newton, p. 24.

"When we consider a project, we really study it - not just the surface idea, but every thing about it. And when we go into that new project, we believe in it all the way. We have confidence in our ability to do it right. And we work hard to do the best possible job." Walt Disney, from *The Innovation Managers Desk Reference,* Paul R. Williams.

Part 6. Delivering The Innovative Product

" I have little patience with scientists who take a board of wood, look for the thinnest part, and drill a great number of holes where the drilling is easy." Albert Einstein, quoted by Philpp Frank in *"Einstein's Philosophy of Science,"* Reviews of Modern Physics(1949).

"We're gambling on our vision, and we would rather do that than make "me too" products. Let some other companies do that. For us, it's always the next dream." Steve Jobs, Interview about the release of the Macintosh(January 24, 1984).

"It is not the critic that counts, not the man who points out how the strong man stumbles or where the doer of deeds could have done them better. The credit belongs to the man who is actually in the arena; -- who strives valiantly: who errs -- but who does actually strive to do the deeds." Theodore Roosevelt, from his speech *"Citizenship In A Republic"* Paris, France, April 23, 1910.

"Obstacles cannot crush me. Every obstacle yields to stern resolve." Leonardo da Vinci, from *The Notebooks of Leonardo da Vinci* (Richter, 1888).

"Speak softly and carry a big stick; you will go far." Theodore Roosevelt, speech, Minnesota State Fair, Sept. 2, 1901.

"People kindly said that I inspired the nation. It was the nation -- that had the lion heart. I had the luck to be called upon to give the roar." Sir Winston Churchill, Speech at the Palace of Westminster, Nov. 30, 1954.

"Be ready to revise any system, scrap any method, abandon any theory, if the success of the job requires it." Henry Ford, *Ford News,* page 2, Jan. 15, 1923, from the Benson Ford Research Center.

"Any featherhead can have confidence in times off victory, but the test is to have faith when things are going wrong." Sir Winston Churchill, from speech to closed war session of the House of Commons, quoted in Life Magazine article, Jan. 28, 1946, p. 29.

"Since new developments are the products of a creative mind, we must therefore stimulate and encourage that type of mind in every way possible." George Washington Carver, article written for The Peanut Journal, from the book, *George Washington Carver In His Own Words,* by Gary R. Kremer.

"These are the times that try men's soul: The summer soldier and the sunshine patriot will, in this crisis, shrink from the service of his country." Thomas Paine "The American Crisis , number 1, 1776.

Part 7. Attributes That Enable A Leader

"A human being is a part of the whole, called by us "The Universe," a part limited in time and space. Our task must be to free ourselves -- by widening our circle of compassion to embrace all living creatures and the whole of nature in its beauty." Albert Einstein, quoted in H. Eves *Mathematical Circles Adieu (Boston 1977).*

"You have to trust in something --- your gut, destiny, life, karma, whatever. This approach has never let me down, and it has made all the difference in my life." Steve Jobs, Address at Stanford University (June 12, 2005).

"Excellence is never an accident. It is always the result of high intention, sincere effort, and intelligent execution ,it represents the wise choice of many alternatives - choice, not chance, determines your destiny." Aristotle, from www.goodreads.com.

"If I were to say to my fellow citizens, that we shall send to the moon -- a giant rocket almost 300 feet tall -- made of new metal alloys, some of which have not yet been invented, -- fitted together with a precision better than the finest watch, -- and then return it safely to earth, -- and do it first before this

decade is out -- then we must be bold ." John F. Kennedy speech, Rice University, September 12, 1962.

"I speak without exaggeration when I say I have constructed 3,000 different theories in connection with the electric light, -- Yet only in two cases did my experiments prove the truth of my theory." Thomas Edison, *Talks With Edison,* by George P. Lathrop, in Harper's magazine, Vol. 80(Feb. 1890), p. 425.

"Diligence is the mother of good luck." Benjamin Franklin, *Poor Richard's Almanack,* (1736).

" Opportunity is missed by most people because it is dressed in overalls and looks like work." Thomas Edison, as quoted in *An Enemy Called Average (1990),* by John L. Mason, p. 55.

"The price of liberty is eternal vigilance." Thomas Jefferson, reported in the *Richmond Enquirer,* Dec. 30, 1834.

"Victory at all costs, victory in spite of all terror, victory however long and hard the road might be; for without victory there is no survival." Sir Winston Churchill speech in the House of Commons, May 13, 1940.

" If you once forfeit the confidence of your fellow citizens, you can never regain their respect and esteem." Abraham Lincoln, speech at Clinton, Illinois, September 8, 1854.

Part 8. Actions & Behaviors Define The Leader

" I swing big with everything I've got. I hit big or I miss big. I like to live as big as I can." Babe Ruth, quoted in *Go For The Gold: Thoughts On Achieving Your Personal Best (2001),*By Ariel Books.

"When eagles are silent, the parrots begin to jabber."
Sir Winston Churchill, letter to Lord Boothby on the India
crisis, from the book *The Last Lion,* by William Manchester, p.
847.

*"If we don't change our direction, we are likely to end up where
we are headed."* Chinese Proverb.

*" His cardinal mistake is that he isolates himself, and allows
nobody to see him; and by which he does not know what is
going on in the very matter he is dealing with."* Abraham
Lincoln relieves General Fremont on September 9, 1861. From
"Lincoln on Leadership," by D. Phillips.

*"The important thing is to not stop questioning. -- One cannot
help but be in awe when he contemplates the mysteries of
eternity, of life, of the marvelous structure of reality. -- never
lose a holy curiosity."* Albert Einstein, from a statement to
William Miller, as quoted in Life Magazine, May 2, 1955.

*"Let us never negotiate out of fear but let us never fear to
negotiate."* John F. Kennedy, Inaugural Address, Jan. 20,
1961.

*"When angry, count to ten before you speak; if very angry, one
hundred."* Thomas Jefferson, letter to Cornelia Jefferson
Randolph, Thomas Jefferson papers University of Virginia.

*"The pursuit of truth does not permit violence on one's
opponent."* Mahatma Gandhi, from his Satyagraha Concept.

*"Politics are almost as exciting as war, and - quite as
dangerous. -- In war you can only be killed once, but in politics
many times."* Sir Winston Churchill" conversation with Harold
Begbie, as cited in *Master Workers*, Begbie, Methuen & Co.
(1906) p. 177.

"Most Fellows try a few things and quit, I never quit till I get what I'm after. That's the only difference between me, that supposed to be lucky, and the fellows that think their unlucky." Thomas Edison, from *Edison Inventing The Century* by Neil Baldwin, p.296.

Part 9.   Working On Self Improvement

"Most people search high and wide for the keys to success. If they only knew, the key to their dreams lies within." George Washington Carver, from *Book of African American Quotations"* edited by Joslyn Pine.

"There are three things extremely hard: steel, a diamond, and to know one's self." Benjamin Franklin, *Poor Richard's Almanack*(1750).

"We must have -- above all confidence in ourselves. We must believe that we are gifted for something, and that this thing, at whatever the cost, must be obtained." Marie Curie, from *Madame Curie, A Biography* (1937) by Eve Curie Labouisse.

"There are people who make things happen, there are people who watch things happen, and there are people who wonder what happened." Proverb.

" I think and think for months and years. Ninety nine times the conclusion is false. The hundred time I am right." Albert Einstein, as quoted in Kantha, *An Einstein Dictionary,* p. 176.

"It would be possible to transmit sounds of any sort if we could only occasion a variation in the intensity of the current exactly like that occurring in the density of air while a given sound is made." Alexander Graham Bell, from Dictionary of Canadian Biography Vol. XV, www.biographi.ca.

" I have but one lamp by which my feet are guided; and that is the lamp of experience." Patrick Henry speech on the Stamp Act, Virginia Convention.

"Wisdom is not a product of schooling but of the lifelong attempt to acquire it." Albert Einstein, from a letter to an admirer, March 22, 1954, quoted in Dukas and Hoffmann, Albert Einstein, the Human Side, P44.

" We hold these truths to be self-evident; that all men are created equal; that they are endowed by their creator with certain unalienable rights; that among these are life, liberty, and the pursuit of happiness, --" Thomas Jefferson, from the Declaration of Independence, July 4, 1776.

" Try to become not a man of success, but try rather to become a man of value." Albert Einstein, from a statement to William Miller, as quoted in Life Magazine, May 2, 1955.

"The more one does and sees and feels, the more one is able to do. Amelia Earhart, from *A Biography of Amelia Earhart* (1939), by George Palmer Putman, p83.

Part 10. Projecting The Future

"It is difficult to say what is impossible, for the dream of yesterday is the hope of today and the reality of tomorrow." Robert Goddard, from his high school graduation oration, *On Taking Things for Granted, 1904.*

"Anything one man can imagine other men can make real." Jules Verne, from his book, *Around The World In 80 Days.*

"It's important to imagine the demands of each generation and accordingly, to work looking ten years into the future. You have

to face the future and think what will be important or necessary at that time." Akio Morita, *The Saying of Akio Morita,* published by Sony Magazines.

"We must dare to be great; and we must realize that greatness is the fruit of toil and sacrifice and high courage." Theodore Roosevelt, speech at the opening of the gubernatorial campaign N.Y.C. (October 5, 1898).

"Courage is the main quality of leadership -- Usually it implies some risk -- especially in new undertakings. Courage to initiate something and to keep it going, pioneering and adventurous spirit to blaze new ways." Walt Disney, from *The Disney Way Field Book(2000),* by Bill Capodadli and Lynn Jackson.

"For some time I have been pestering -- to let me set up an experimental department where designers and shop artisans could work together closely in the development of airplanes without the delays and complications of intermediate departments --." Clarence L. *"Kelly"* Johnson (founder of the Lockheed Skunk Works), from the book Kelly, More Than My Share of It All, By Clarence L. *"Kelly"* Johnson with Maggie Smith.

"Houston, Tranquility Base here, The Eagle has landed." -- That's one small step for man, one giant leap for mankind." Neil Armstrong, The New York Times front page July 21 1969, reporting on the first moon landing by Apollo 11(July 20, 1969).

"I have not the smallest molecule of faith in aerial navigation other than ballooning." Lord Kelvin response to a request to join the Aeronautical Society, December 8, 1896.

" I began to feel that I lived on a higher plane than the skeptics of the ground; one that was richer because of its very association with the element of danger -- In flying I tasted the

144

wine of the Gods of which they could know nothing." Charles A. Lindbergh, *The Spirit Of St. Louis*(1953).

"The only limit to our realization of tomorrow will be our doubts of today." Franklin Roosevelt, undelivered address prepared for Jefferson Day, April 13, 1945.

"Happiness lies not in the mere possession of money, it lies in the joy of achievement, in the thrill of creative effort." Franklin Roosevelt, Inaugural speech, March 4, 1933.

Epilogue

"No individual has any right to come into the world and go out of it with out leaving behind -- distinct and legitimate reasons for having passed through it." George Washington Carver, from the Introduction to the book, *George Washington Carver In His Own Words,* by Gary R. Kremer.

Photo Credits

All of the pictures of birds in this book were taken by the author and his wife, Janice Noehren Chaplin. They were almost entirely taken in the Cape Cod National Seashore, in the lakes and forested areas of New England, and along the California coast and in desert areas inland. The cameras that were used extensively were Canon DSLR's with 200mm and 300mm Canon telephoto lens, combined with 1.4x and 2x extenders.

The picture of the Andromeda Galaxy (M031) was taken by the author in Connecticut, with a TMB 80mm refractor, mounted piggyback on a Celestron C14 telescope and German equatorial mount, using a modified Canon 50D camera.